To Make a Difference

MERCER
UNIVERSITY PRESS

Endowed by

TOM WATSON BROWN

and

THE WATSON-BROWN FOUNDATION, INC.

To Make a Difference

James T. McAfee, Jr.

By Scott Walker

MERCER UNIVERSITY PRESS | Macon, Georgia
35 Years of Publishing Excellence

MUP/ H897

Published by Mercer University Press, Macon, Georgia 31207

1400 Coleman Avenue
Macon, Georgia 31207

9 8 7 6 5 4 3 2 1

Books published by Mercer University Press are printed on acid-free paper that meets the requirements of the American National Standard for Information Sciences—Permanence of Paper for Printed Library Materials.

Library of Congress Cataloging-in-Publication Data

Walker, Scott, 1950- , author.
To make a difference : James T. McAfee, Jr. / by Scott Walker.
p. ; cm.
Includes index.
ISBN 978-0-88146-513-6 (hardback : alk. paper) -- ISBN 0-88146-513-5 (hardback : alk. paper)
I. Title.
[DNLM: 1. McAfee, James T., Jr (James Thomas), 1939-2004.
2. Hospital Administrators--Georgia--Biography.
3. Entrepreneurship--Georgia--Biography. 4. Health Care Sector--Georgia. WZ 100]
RA971
362.11068092--dc23
[B]

2014035259

Contents

Foreword

R. Kirby Godsey

Every person's life is a story. No one enters or exits the stage of human history as an isolated, disconnected event. We are all shaped by the people and events that precede us, and we, in turn, leave indelible marks on those whose lives are nurtured and influenced by our presence. We belong to an ever-flowing stream. Each of us lives in this moving stream of history, and the course of this stream is inevitably and unalterably changed because we have come onto history's stage.

James T. McAfee, Jr., who I knew and loved simply as Jim, bears testimony that he, like all of us, was a child of his history. William Faulkner reminded us that, "The past is never dead. It's not even past." One of the marks of Jim's remarkable story was that he gladly embraced and celebrated the important landmarks of his life. His own inner character developed within an arena filled with a wide range of emotions and nurturing, from a father's stern love, which could hardly be spoken, to a mother's love, which was so embracing, so affirming, that words were unnecessary. All of Jim's achievements grew out from this youthful terrain, which combined these high and uncompromising expectations with an unconditional, affirming compassion. This rather rare combination shows up throughout his life and work, and it was a principal driver that enabled Jim McAfee to make a dramatic difference in business, to be a larger-than-life patriarch in his family, and, through his philanthropy, to change the course of historic institutions.

The rising tide of Jim's presence in the ever-flowing stream of history changed people's lives and the direction and profitability of enterprises as he molded the emerging mission of institutions that received his favor and affirmation. Many people have genuine compassion. Many people embrace the rigor, even the sternness, of high expectations. Rarely, however, are these gifts lived so fully or wisely bound together as in the life and work of Jim McAfee.

Jim McAfee was not a simple man. He was complex to the core. He was adored, but feared. He was affirming, but demanding. He was generous, but frugal. He was hopeful, but realistic. He believed, but he doubted. He was laser-focused, but kept an eye out for new opportunities. He was a faithful steward of the church, but could also be the church's sharp critic.

Jim's relationships were also complex. He was devoted to his family, both to the family that nurtured him as well as to the family he nurtured. Being with family, taking care of family, and directing family decisions remained central to his sense of purpose. Though devoted to his family with an unrelenting passion, Jim sometimes held the bar of expectations so high for family members that they may, on occasions, have experienced his admonitions as unaffirming. Beyond his family, he was engaged in complex business relationships that stretched from his initial steps into hospital administration to his emergence as a leading player in major hospital corporations and his oversight of a major corporate healthcare turnaround. His complex business and corporate endeavors were always marked by both discipline and care. If Jim set a goal, achieving it was the only option. He never entertained the thought of failing, and he made this expectation clear to every person that worked around him or who lived with him. Do it right. Do it with integrity. But get it done. Failure was not an option.

The strokes of destiny that brought my life into cadence with Jim McAfee's life and career were largely displayed on the canvas of Mercer University. Jim believed in education. Jim also believed in Baptist's engagement in education, so long as this engagement was not used to contradict reason or compromise the search for truth. He was confident that critical and rigorous thought was no threat to faith.

Jim and I often talked deep into the night about issues of thinking and believing and the inevitable tension between education and organized religion. We shared a profound respect for intellectual freedom along with a respect for religious diversity. Jim ultimately translated his commitment to rigorous thinking and unconditional compassion into shaping a new agenda for Mercer University that underscored this devotion to disciplined thought alongside thoughtful piety.

Jim would have run from any appellations of piety, but in reality, Jim McAfee was a deeply pious man. And out of these streams of piety and thoughtful reflection, Jim along with his wife, Carolyn, helped Mercer University to form a sustainable School of Theology, which now bears their name. Their deep sense of purpose, their devotion to preserving the bond between thought and faith, and their commitment to religious freedom consistently guided their giving.

As we read the story of Jim McAfee, we should remember the counsel of William Faulkner. The past is never dead. I cannot think of anyone who is more alive than James T. McAfee, Jr. He lives in the family he bred. He lives in the businesses he conceived. He lives in the influence among colleagues he nurtured. He lives in the institutions he shaped. He embodied deep within his soul both discipline and compassion, and he gathered these twin gifts from his childhood and used them to transform the world around him in a way that made an enduring difference for many people and places.

Chapter 1

Early Years, 1739–1932

Lost In Time

Most Americans whose ancestors emigrated to the United States prior to the American Revolutionary War have lost the trail that connects them to their past. Few know the names of their forebears who first set foot on North American shores. Fewer still can recount the long and fascinating story of how each ensuing generation traveled, settled, toiled, and persevered to arrive at the present moment. There is much in every family's history that is lost in time.

Though much fact and detail has faded in the lineage of James T. McAfee, Jr., Jim often recounted the family lore that his McAfee ancestors were part of the heralded McAfee clan that settled the primal land of Kentucky with Daniel Boone. Though this is likely true, centuries earlier this particular clan of McAfees was originally established on the island of Colonsay, just off the west coast of Scotland. In 1645, John McAfee, Sr., moved his family from this remote island to the mainland of Scotland and settled near Glasgow. Then in 1672, lured by an attractive offer of land, he again moved, this time to County Armagh, Ireland, along with his twenty-seven-year-old son, John McAfee, Jr. Sixty-seven years later, in 1739, James McAfee, Sr., the son of John McAfee, Jr., emigrated with his wife, Jane, from Ireland to New Castle County, Delaware. Thus was established the McAfee clan in the "New World" and in "New England."

Prior to the American Revolutionary War, the McAfees departed New England and settled briefly in Lancaster, Pennsylvania, then wandered through Virginia and North Carolina, and ultimately became some of the first European settlers to explore the lush country that Native Americans called *Kanta-ke*.[1] By 1775, four McAfee brothers—James, Robert, William, and Samuel—had cleared land and built log cabins in what is now Mercer County, Kentucky. It is this clan of McAfees who slumber and sleep in the family tradition that entranced young Jim McAfee as a little boy.[2]

William Cleveland McAfee:
"A Gentleman's Agreement"

When mythic mists lift and the light of day shines on the twentieth century, we find Jim McAfee's grandfather, William Cleveland McAfee, having recently moved to Dyer County, Tennessee and signing his name on a 1910 federal census form. William is twenty-five years old and married to twenty-six year old Hattie M. McAfee. Both William and Hattie testify that they were born in Tennessee. In less than a decade of marriage, five children were also born to this young couple; three lived to adulthood and two died as infants. William's and Hattie's youthful faces were creased by both joy and sorrow.[3]

Dyer County is located in the northwest corner of Tennessee, adjacent to the Mississippi River, and slightly south of the western tip of Kentucky. Though the town of Dyersburg is the county seat, William McAfee settled his family on a farm near the tiny crossroads hamlet of Tigrett. While continuing the McAfee pilgrimage westward, William was tentatively sinking roots into new land that perched on the edge of the "wide-river divide" of the North American continent. Should he want to move further west, he could cross the Mississippi River and settle in Arkansas, twenty miles due west, or in Missouri, thirty miles northwest. Though his Tennessee-Kentucky heritage constrained him for the moment, he was perched to move quickly.[4]

However, good fortune soon grew from the dark Tennessee river-bottom soil that William farmed in Dyer County. Within ten years he had earned enough crop money to buy a cotton gin and invest in a profitable timber business. As his two daughters, Ruby and Beatrice, and his baby son, James, formed their early memories, they recalled days of security and prosperity. William's life was full of hard labor but also good living and a promising future.

William and Hattie were also people of deep religious faith. They introduced their children to Bible stories and took them to church. When their small congregation in Tigrett built a new sanctuary, William and Hattie gave a parcel of their farmland for the church site. Christian faith and community were an integral part of their lives, and it was faith that would sustain them when life became hard and difficult.

As the children grew older, two traumatic events shattered their secure, prosperous lives. The first came as a result of William seeking to enhance his income by investing in speculative ventures "out west." A friend had crossed the Mississippi and settled in the emerging oil field region of Oklahoma. Writing to William, he described the "once-in-a-life-time" opportunity to invest in oil production. Soon William withdrew a significant portion of his savings from the bank to join in a partnership with his friend to purchase an oil well. No contracts were signed or promissory notes written; it was simply a gentleman's agreement and sealed with a firm handshake.

Though his friend was honest and the initial revenue from the oil production was profitable, there was one thing that William's partner had not foreseen—his own early death. Upon hearing of his partner's demise, William attempted to legally formalize his partnership in the oil well. However, his partner's widow denied all knowledge of William's loan or a gentleman's agreement. A lengthy and costly court battle ensued, but William ultimately lost his investment, his confidence, and his optimism. As the Great Depression era then descended upon the nation, crushing farmers and ranchers, he floundered and sought desperately to survive financially.

When Christmas of that same fateful year approached, a second event seared their family memories. All three of William and Hattie's children were now teenagers, and although Christmas was meager, it was rich in spirit. Nestled by the hearth for warmth, someone smelled smoke floating into the room. Suddenly the house erupted into flames. With no fire department in Tigrett, the McAfee house burned rapidly to the ground. There was no insurance, and they lost everything.

William McAfee was never able to emotionally heal or financially recover from this time of loss. Eking out a living through the Great Depression years, William continued to farm. He also supplemented his income by working as an automotive salesman, trying to capitalize on America's new love affair with Henry Ford's horseless carriage.[5] But William was unable to return to the lucrative days he had experienced before the oil-well fiasco. His large tract of land became unmanageable without financial means to purchase equipment, fertilizer, seed, and additional labor. Simply feeding his family each day became his sole focus.

Later in life, William and Hattie moved to Greenville, Mississippi, to live with his oldest daughter, Ruby, and her husband, Thomas Stallings, who owned a successful funeral home. Thomas was a good and gentle man who loved and supported his in-laws. He soon purchased a general store for William to manage in his retirement years. A meaningful job kept William busy and healthy.

Living in the poorest state in the South and watching hungry people stare at the produce and canned goods on his shelves, William felt deep empathy for his neighbors. He often extended credit to families he knew were considered poor risks. He could not refuse a hungry person food, and he would not deny the right of anyone to have a sense of dignity. Increasingly the bold teachings of Jesus became real to him and compassion became more important than profit. Gradually, his generosity led to bankruptcy. He literally "gave the store away."[6] Until he died in 1956 at age eighty-four, William McAfee continued to help his neighbors who were in need.

Years later, William's grandson, Jim McAfee, often reflected on his grandfather's difficult life. Jim gleaned two lessons that shaped his own future: First, always use sound business practices and do not take undue risks. And second, give generously to people in need and to causes that are worthy. This was the legacy that William Cleveland McAfee bequeathed to his grandson. It was a legacy worth far more than financial inheritance.[7]

James T. McAfee: "This Won't Happen Again!"

William McAfee's only son, James Thomas McAfee, was also greatly shaped by the financial struggles that dogged his father. Born in 1907 and soon nicknamed "JT," he was an intense and headstrong young man who wanted to change his situation. Yet, throughout his ensuing eighty-nine years he never resolved the hurt and grief of being snatched out of the comfortable and stable existence of his early childhood and thrust into poverty, struggle, and shame.

Rarely would JT speak about his past. It was a throbbing pain he kept suppressed. But on occasion he would recount the story of the frigid winter morning when he walked around the smoldering wreckage of his family's burned farmhouse, seeking to find anything of value. Suddenly his young eyes focused on a pair of wool mittens he had been given for Christmas. Snatching them from the edge of the ash mound, he tried to pull them over his cold hands. He quickly discovered the mittens were too singed to be worn. Tossing them back into the ashes, he walked away, determined that he would not allow his own life to devolve into such tragic loss again. But his emotional scars never healed. Later, as an adult, he was driven to control and constrain his money, his family, and his destiny. Frugality became a way of life, and he resolved, "I got taken once but this won't happen again!"[8]

As JT moved from childhood into adolescence, he became a strong and athletic young man. Not particularly tall or large in stature, he still loved to play baseball and football. Later in adulthood, he spent many Saturday afternoons listening to the blaring of two televisions and three radios, eagerly keeping up with all of the scores in college and professional sports. JT was competitive, driven, and active. And sports were a way to win, compete, and hope again.

Yet, there was another side of JT that also longed to be pampered and cared for. Being the youngest of three children, he was spoiled by his mother and sisters. He soon expected to be "king of the house" and to "rule the roost," traits he carried into adulthood and his future married life.[9]

As JT approached high school graduation in 1925, he dreamed of becoming a physician, but the expense of college and medical school were beyond his means. Instead, he decided to join the army and be trained as a medic. Perhaps this could be the first step toward a medical career. Shortly after graduation, he talked to an army recruiter, signed on the dotted line, and was soon in boot camp at Fort Benning, Georgia, exhausted, homesick, and miserable.

JT quickly discovered that Uncle Sam's army was not for him. The military was radically downsizing following World War I, and JT took the first opportunity to take early leave of the army with an honorable discharge. Though his medical dreams were dimming, he refused to go back home to Tigrett and walk in the ruts of old paths again. Rather, he traveled to Memphis, Tennessee, to live with his older sister, Beatrice, who was single and working for the Dixie Greyhound Lines. He found temporary work at a Gulf Oil station until he could discern his vocational path. Within a short time, he stumbled into the job that would form his lifelong career.[10]

In the late 1920s, communication by telephone was quickly evolving and radically changing American business and society. While many homes did not have a telephone, it was clear that within a short time, the telephone industry would be a dominant technological force within the American economy. JT learned that there was an urgent need for young men to be trained by telephone companies in basic electronics. The prospect of becoming a doctor suddenly seemed less beguiling, and JT found the opportunity to become a telephone technician instead.

After completing training as a technician, JT was transferred from Memphis to Chattanooga, Tennessee, to install newly developed dial-switching equipment. He was assigned to help central telephone offices transition from operator assisted switchboard calls to direct-dial calling. Little did he know that he would soon fall in love with a telephone operator named Frances Zoe Hilliard.[11]

The Hilliard Clan: "The End of Wanderlust"

Frances Hilliard had her own fascinating story to tell of the bonds of strong family love amidst spiraling poverty and struggle. Like the McAfees, the Hilliards were early English settlers in North America. With each generation they had moved to a new state, seeking another new beginning and one more fresh start. Seemingly, their wanderlust could not be quenched.

The earliest existent Hilliard memories shine on the dim figure of Philemon Hilliard who was born in Virginia in 1752. As tension between the adolescent American colonies and "Mother England" intensified, Philemon moved south across the Virginia border to the greater safety of Warren County, North Carolina. Shortly after making this move, he married Martha Glen Buford and began to plow North Carolina soil.

Two decades later, Philemon and Martha's son, John William Hilliard, began himself to experience that restlessness that was in the blood, and he was lured across the North Carolina state line to South Carolina by the wiles of one Elizabeth Rogers. Upon their marriage, they settled in Camden, South Carolina, in the turbulent aftermath of the Revolutionary War. Formerly occupied by the British army, the area surrounding Camden suffered one of the worst American defeats of the revolution. Though the Revolutionary War had now ended, this region of South Carolina still seethed with enmity between patriots and former Tories.

When John Hilliard's first son was born in Camden in 1809, John honored his father with a namesake, Philemon Burford Hilliard. Twenty years later, "Philemon the Younger" was the next to succumb to the clan wanderlust, leaving the low-country, colonial heritage of Kershaw County, South Carolina, and moving into the back-country wilderness of the southern Appalachian frontier. Settling in Tennessee in his early twenties, Philemon married Emily Manning, and she soon bore the first of ten children.

Ever restless, Philemon and Emily finally settled their brood in the Cherokee lands of Madison County, Alabama. Nestled in the north-central region of Alabama, this land is cradled by the looping Tennessee River and composed of lush, rolling hills that gradually ascend to the southern range of the Appalachian Mountains. By 1811, the city of Huntsville had been founded in Madison County, slowly becoming a center of commerce in northern Alabama. Philemon and Emily finally let roots grow deep near the tiny hamlet of Monrovia, 15 miles northwest of Huntsville.

Building a cabin, Philemon chopped down trees, dug up stumps, and cleared virgin land to start a small farm. By the time Philemon's son, Joseph Whitfield Hilliard, was born in 1834, the Hilliards had bought African slaves to bear the brunt of backbreaking labor and expand their tillable acreage. Philemon and his sons soon developed a large, profitable farm and built a country store.

Philemon lived a long life and watched his sons and daughters grow into adulthood in Alabama. Born only twenty-three years after the final battle of the American Revolutionary War had been fought on the banks of the Combahee River in his native South Carolina, Philemon now entered old age with anxious eyes as the inevitability of the American Civil War loomed. Constant change and conflict had tracked every step of his nomadic life.

As the fateful decade of the 1860s began, Philemon's son Joseph moved out of his father's house and onto farmland near his family's homestead. Marrying Betty Wall and nurturing a young marriage, Joseph resisted joining the Confederate army in the early years of the war, but by 1863, with Southern defeats at Vicksburg and Gettysburg, every able-bodied Southern man was expected to join up. At age twenty-nine, Joseph signed the roster of the 26th Alabama Infantry Regiment and went to war, leaving his pregnant wife to bear their first child alone.[12]

Over the next eighteen months, the 26th Alabama Regiment endured savage fighting at the Battle of Atlanta, slaughter on the killing grounds of Franklin, Tennessee, and the disastrous collapse of the Confederate army of Tennessee at the Battle of Nashville on 16 December 1864. During the ensuing Confederate retreat from Nashville, spanning the Christmas week of 1864, the 26th Alabama Regiment was assigned to General John Bell Hood's rear guard. This small unit was given the suicidal task of protecting the rear of the fleeing Confederate army as it rushed south to enter the sanctuary of northern Alabama. This mad dash was also in the midst of the most severe winter of the nineteenth century, and many soldiers did not have shoes, coats, or rations. Incredibly, the grueling forced march was successful, and it led Joseph Hilliard back across the Tennessee River and within "spitting distance" of his farm in Monrovia.

With the surrender of the Confederate army of Tennessee a few months later on April 26, 1865, Private Joseph M. Hilliard trudged back home, never to leave again. The family wanderlust was gone, depleted by the relentless marches and battles of a ghastly Civil War.

William Larkin Hilliard

While Joseph was fighting in Tennessee in 1864, Joseph's wife, Betty, gave birth to a son, William Larkin Hilliard, who would become the grandfather of James T. McAfee, Jr. As William Larkin grew to adulthood in the post-Civil War South, he proved to be quite unlike his forebears. He was not a pioneer, had little wanderlust, lacked business acumen, and disliked farming. But he did have a deep hunger for education. When he enrolled as an older teenager at the fledgling University of Alabama, he became the first person of his direct Hilliard lineage to attend college.

When William returned to Monrovia after his studies at the University of Alabama, he was employed by the Monrovia community as a school teacher. In his early twenties, he fell in love with Frances (Fannie) McKenzie, a young teenager seven years younger than he. After a short courtship they were married in 1887, when William was twenty-three and Fannie just sixteen. Soon after their marriage, William stopped teaching school and partnered with his father, Joseph, in farming and small business ventures.

A year after their wedding, in 1888, Fannie bore their first child, a son named Clarence Donaldson Hilliard. It would be eighteen more years until Fannie gave birth to their second child, Edna Mae, in 1906. Their final child, Frances Zoe, was born in 1909. Clarence and his younger sisters were nearly a generation apart.

As an adult, William Larkin Hilliard was perhaps a bit eccentric. Even though he was studious, intellectual and had attended the University of Alabama, he did not enroll his three children in school beyond the third grade. Clarence, Edna, and Frances were bright, intelligent, and learned to read and write, but for reasons known only to himself, their school-teacher father did not place a high priority on the education of his own children. Rather, amidst post-Civil War poverty and reconstruction, they learned from an early age to work and support the family farm.

William's son, Clarence, was married in his early twenties to Anna Beatrice Smith. In the mid-1920s, Clarence and Anna left the struggling family farm in Madison County, Alabama, and moved to Chattanooga, Tennessee, seeking better employment opportunities. As they entered into the Great Depression years and the second decade of their marriage, they suddenly had twelve children to feed and care for. Clarence found work with the Southern Railroad and also had a second job as a paymaster for the Civilian Conservation Corps (CCC).

However, back in Alabama, family affairs were deteriorating, and Clarence became increasingly concerned about his father, William Larkin, and his two young sisters. Clarence's mother, Fannie, had recently died at the age of forty-six from chronic illness, leaving William Larkin a widower at fifty-three with two daughters aged eleven and eight. A year later, William's father, Joseph, also died, and William was forced to take on heavy farming responsibilities and a country general store. With the loss of his wife and father still fresh, two young daughters to raise, and his only son away in Chattanooga, William began to flounder.

Inheriting a portion of his father's land, William soon proved that he was not a farmer. He was friendly, gregarious, and kind—attributes that better suited him to running the general store than raising profitable crops. He loved people and was generous to a fault. He continually extended credit to customers in need and soon faced serious financial troubles in the midst of the worst economic depression in American history.

In Chattanooga, Clarence looked on with alarm at his father in Alabama and knew he had to do something for his two younger sisters, Edna and Frances, as they neared their vulnerable teenage years. Even though Clarence had twelve children, lived in a four-room house, did not own a car, and was working two jobs, he and Bea insisted that William Larkin close the bankrupt store, sell what was left of the farm, and come live with them in Chattanooga. In 1924, William loaded up Edna and Frances on a train and all three traveled east to Chattanooga with little more than the clothing in their suitcases. They moved in with Clarence, and the motherless girls were soon calling Clarence's wife, "Aunt Bea."

As the Great Depression deepened, Clarence rose at 5:30 every morning to walk to work in the railroad yards. He came home in the evening to continue laboring with his young sons to extend the size of their small house, now bursting at the seams with family and children. Soon a four-room house became a six-room house with one small bathroom. When three adults and 14 children bedded down for the night, it was a close community. Clarence's son, "CD" Hilliard, recalls that in winter, sleeping in the thin-walled back room, he would often wake up with flakes of frost covering his handmade quilts. But CD also remembers that the drafty house was always neat and cozy and adequate for their needs. The depth of their family love did more than the struggling old stove to keep the children warm in winter. The Hilliards possessed something money could not buy: a close and caring family.

Unfortunately, William Larkin's daughters, Edna and Frances, did not have the luxury of going back to school when they reached Chattanooga. Everyone needed to work. Frances was only eight when her mother died and twelve when she moved to Chattanooga. Drifting down the streets of Chattanooga and desperately searching for employment, she walked into a soda shop and "lied about her age" to land her first job dipping ice cream.

However, within a few years, Frances Hilliard left the soda shop and found secure employment with the local telephone company as a switchboard operator. This job not only connected her to security and benefits, but it introduced her to her future husband as well.[13]

The McAfees Meet the Hilliards

Far to the west in Memphis, Tennessee, with the 1930s underway, JT McAfee had completed his training as a telephone technician. He was soon transferred to the Chattanooga telephone district to upgrade their switchboard system to accommodate direct-dial telephones. One of the real advantages of this job for a young, single man was being in contact with many beautiful women who were telephone operators. One of these operators was a lovely and affectionate young woman named Frances Hilliard.

Frances Hilliard was pretty, with flowing auburn hair and a soft, alluring countenance. She was gentle, quiet, neat, and lady-like. Having endured much hardship and adjustment in her youth, she exuded a maturity and wisdom that was both attractive and reassuring. Frances was a woman who was warm and compassionate but who could be counted on to endure and prevail when things became difficult.[14]

JT was a vigorous burst of energy when he descended upon Chattanooga in his early twenties. He was a young man with his "first real job" and was determined to do well. He soon met Jimmy Harding who was dating Anna Laura Hilliard, one of Clarence Hilliard's brood of a dozen children. Jimmy quickly made arrangements for JT to meet Anna Laura's youngest aunt, Frances Hilliard. A romance was sparked, and generations merged together. Centuries of constant movement, westward travel, a revolutionary war and civil war, success and failure, lost oil wells and failed country stores, had all conspired to bring the McAfees and Hilliards together. Life is a process of irony and coincidence, of fate and chance and luck and fortune all bound together. And, yes, of grace and goodness, too.

Chapter 2

Chattanooga and Childhood, 1932–1945

James T. McAfee and Frances Zoe Hilliard were married in Chattanooga on September 1, 1932. Joining their lives together at the height of America's Great Depression, they shared much love but few financial resources. They were grateful to have stable employment with the telephone company and were able to move into their first house on Woods Drive.

Fourteen months later, Frances gave birth to a healthy and vigorous little boy. JT named his first born in honor of his father, William C. McAfee, which pleased the old man greatly. With Bill's birth, JT and Frances grew into full adulthood with all of its responsibilities.

In the first months of every marriage many themes and scripts from childhood and age-old family traditions emerge and are woven into a thick and complex fabric of family communication and interaction. JT was a strong, male figure and expected to be the man of the house. He wanted his home to be his castle and to have the final word on family decisions. He was dominant, firm, and as the youngest child in his family, accustomed to having his way.[1]

Frances was also the youngest child in her family. However, far from being demanding, she was quiet, courteous, and gentle. She played her role as mother, cook, seamstress, nurse, administrator and comforter—the traditional 1930s American housewife. Growing up within the community of the large Hilliard clan, she was bred to think not of herself but of others, to work toward compromise and compatibility. Like her father, she was generous, kind, and willing to help a stranger. Yet, behind her gentleness there was rock-hard strength. She was a survivor. And, she was a lady.

Early in their marriage, some of the traits of JT's childhood struggle came to the fore. Like many children who weathered the Great Depression, he was determined that he would not fall into financial ruin, as his father had done, and that he would hold tightly to the family purse strings. Frugality would be his watchword. Budgets and financial decisions were his alone to make and control. Frances was given an allowance to fund household operations and her own personal expenses. But JT resolutely clenched the purse. Such fiscal dominance would become his source of power, and at times, his method of manipulation.

JT's strength and intensity combined with Frances's gentleness and pliable nature usually produced a comfortable balance and compatibility. But this same combination of traits could also result in simmering tension and quiet resentment. The character and personality of a marriage relationship can never be clearly seen prior to the marriage vows, and JT and Frances were discovering the nuances of each other.

The young McAfee family, however, was primarily healthy and stable. From the beginning JT and Frances rooted their family in the life of the Baptist church. Joining Ridgedale Baptist Church in Chattanooga, JT soon became a deacon. Frances was as generous as her husband was frugal and invested her life in helping others. Their children would cut their teeth on the back of church pews and recognize hymn tunes before they spoke words.

As Bill began to walk and then run, JT taught him to throw a baseball, swing a bat, kick a football, and invited him into the athletic world that had been so much a part of his own childhood and youth. Bill had a natural proclivity for sports, and athletics became a means for a father-son relationship to deepen.

Gradually JT advanced through the ranks at the telephone company in Chattanooga. He possessed a good work ethic and the ability to lead. His dreams of medicine had long since dissolved, and he committed his future to institutional advancement and success within the telephone company.

As Bill grew and prepared to enter first grade, Frances gave birth to her second and final child on June 17, 1939. JT and Frances hoped for a girl but the stork brought another blue bundle. JT proudly gave the boy his own name, James Thomas McAfee, Jr. Though usually referred to as James or Jim, the extended family soon nicknamed him "Buddy."

Buddy came by his nickname naturally. He was a chubby and cuddly child with a broad and contagious grin. He was usually happy and cheerful, with bright eyes that crinkled throughout his life when he grinned. His laughter was spontaneous, easily transmitting itself to those around him. Though he could be intense and serious, his primary demeanor was one of being everyone's buddy.

Just as Bill had naturally found closeness and affinity with his father, Jim developed intimacy and acceptance with his mother. She was his place of softness, the one who always offered him comfort and reassurance as he found his way into an often-confusing family dynamic. For all of their lives, Jim and Frances would have a special and unalterable relationship.

As Jim was born, the United States economy remained stagnant and the last stages of the Great Depression lingered. However, military and defense industries were moving into high gear as a worldwide war seemed imminent in both Europe and the Pacific. JT was a thirty-two-year-old married man with two small children and held an important communications job. It was not likely that he would be drafted into military service, but these were uncertain times, and JT sought financial stability.

As war inevitably erupted and strict rationing of certain products began, items such as rubber tires, gasoline, and automobiles became increasingly expensive and scarce. One day a friend made JT a tempting and lucrative offer to buy JT's car. Seeing an opportunity to "flip cars" and make a quick profit, JT immediately accepted. However, after Pearl Harbor and America's declaration of war on both Germany and Japan, the opportunity for citizens to buy new or used cars became nearly impossible. Although JT banked his money, he found himself without an automobile for nearly the duration of the war. Riding the bus every day to work became an onerous chore and one that he resented.

However, young Jim soon became quite enamored with buses, those amazing vehicles that took his Daddy to work every day. Perhaps Jim's first budding vocational dream was to become a bus driver. Jim was ecstatic whenever Frances took him for a bus ride, and "Buddy" soon became friends with the drivers.

One day a kind driver gave Jim a handful of cancelled bus transfers. For a little boy this was a gift greater than gold. Jim quickly began his first business enterprise. His tricycle was miraculously transformed into a city bus. Jim would sell tickets to imaginary passengers, carefully giving them their change, and seating them in invisible rows behind him. For hours Jim delivered these passengers to places in his vivid imagination, stopping his tricycle to bid each one a fond farewell. This was a childhood fantasy. But it was also the birth of life-dreams. Jim's innate business acumen and people skills were finding expression in his preschool world. He was learning to "drive his own bus"! The courage to dream and to have visions of what might be possible was being expressed.

During his preschool years, Jim was also fortunate to know his maternal grandfather, William Larkin Hilliard, better known as "Toddy" by grandchildren and friends. Now in his mid-seventies, old Toddy still lived with his son Clarence. Often on weekend nights

Toddy would gather his great-grandchildren into Clarence's cozy house and mesmerize them with his vast repertoire of stories. He would slip back into his old role of "teacher" and make the world of history come alive and present. Toddy was a true gift to be given and shared with this budding generation.

During the day, Toddy spent his hours ambling along the streets of downtown Chattanooga, greeting folks and selling bags of popcorn and peanuts to passersby. Everyone knew Toddy, and he was a much-loved character. Though he intended to make a buck or two each day, Toddy was quick to give you his popcorn and peanuts for free if you could not buy them. There was a gentleness about this man reminiscent of St. Francis of Assisi. In many ways he was not practical or realistic, but he was well connected to the spirit of God and goodness. Jim saw through a child's eyes that "Blessed are the pure in heart for they shall see God!"[2]

Though securely attached to his mother, Jim struggled to relate to his brother and his father; Bill was nearly six years older than Jim. At the time of Jim's birth, Bill was preparing to enter the first grade, and when Jim later started school, Bill was almost a teenager. It seemed that their worlds were seldom in the same orbit. Bill was physical and athletic and his world revolved around sports. This athletic trait bonded Bill with his father. Jim, however, was not by nature athletic, and this seemed to exclude him from activities that Bill and JT enjoyed together.

Bill also had the strength and tendency to bend his father's rules, and find out how much he could get away with. JT was a firm disciplinarian and, like most fathers of his day, believed in using a wooden paddle, frequently called "the board of education." When Bill would trespass into forbidden behavioral territory, JT would "take a cornstalk to him" and "light a fire under his britches." Jim observed this and decided not to overtly disobey or "step over lines." Jim and

Bill simply had different dispositions and personalities. But they were brothers and ultimately loyal to each other.[3]

In 1932, the first Krystal hamburger restaurant in America opened in Chattanooga. Some of Jim's fondest memories of childhood were when Bill would come home from school, plop Jim on the handlebars of his bicycle, and coast downhill to the famous Krystal to buy hamburgers and orange drinks. As an adult, Jim became a connoisseur of fine food, but nothing would ever beat the childhood taste of Krystal's and the thrill of a bicycle ride with his big brother.

In terms of relating to his father, it remained difficult for Jim to find an avenue for a relationship. Jim also developed an early fear or uneasiness around his father. JT was often loud, outspoken, and had an intensity that was intimidating for a little boy. Jim learned to keep his distance. As Jim approached school age and JT was finally able to buy a car, Jim would often wait for his father to drive home from work. Meeting him at the end of the driveway, Jim could sense his father's mood. If JT was in a good humor, Jim would step up on the running board of the car and his Dad would let him ride up the driveway with him. If he intuited that JT was irritated or edgy, Jim would simply say hello and walk over to a neighbor's house to play. As he once told a young cousin, "I'm afraid of my Daddy."[4]

Though it is now difficult to look back through the clouded lens of time and assess Jim's relationship with his father with complete accuracy, it is clear that Jim's most intimate relationship was with his mother and that his relationship with his father was more strained and distant. Jim would seldom feel that he had his father's blessing, but his mother remained his loyal champion until the day she died.

When Jim was six, his world changed. JT came home one day to announce that he had received a significant promotion and that the family would be moving to Jackson, Tennessee. This move would place the McAfees in western Tennessee again and much closer to

JT's early roots in Tigrett and Dyer County. It would be in Jackson that Jim would spend his most impressionable years.

Chapter 3

At Home in Jackson, Tennessee, 1945–1953

September 1945 was a momentous month for Americans. World War II drew to its final victorious conclusion as surrender documents were signed between Allied forces and the Empire of Japan on the deck of the USS *Missouri* in Tokyo Bay. Thousands of American veterans soon returned home to begin their lives anew and give birth to the Baby Boomer generation.

Jim's childhood world was also radically changing, and his young eyes grew wide as his childhood possessions were loaded into a truck and moved from mountainous Chattanooga to the flat, agrarian land of Jackson, Tennessee. Not only was Jim moving to a new city and neighborhood, but he would also be starting the first grade, a significant rite of passage for American children.

Arriving in Jackson, JT settled his family into a temporary rental dwelling on Glendale Street until a small house could be built.[1] A local contractor, Ellis Maness, soon laid the foundation for the McAfees' house, a one-story brick structure with three bedrooms and one bathroom. The address of 308 West Deaderick Street became the center of Jim's universe until he graduated from college sixteen years later.

Soon, Bill and Jim were helping their father plant grass and maintain the new yard. The yard was flat until it sloped down a steep bank to meet West Deaderick Street. JT was particular about his lawn and taught his sons how to keep it to his specifications. Weeds were pulled up by hand. Johnson grass and nut grass were declared particular enemies. JT insisted on using a manual reel lawn mower and tightened the reel until it was difficult to spin. JT's future grandson, J. Thomas McAfee, III, proudly uses a riding engine-powered reel lawn mower today to manicure his grass. Some traditions span generations.[2]

Child protests aside, Jim's experience of yard work developed an early love for natural beauty, lush lawns, and lovely flower gardens. Though Jim might have bridled under his father's firm supervision, the experience of maintaining a yard spawned a respect for neatness, maintenance, and order. These would be guiding principles in Jim's future business enterprises.

Jim soon made life-long friends in Jackson. One of his childhood buddies, Matt Tomlin, vividly remembers the first time he saw Jim. It was a cold autumn day and the first flurries of snow had fallen. Matt and his buddies were walking down West Deadrick Street "looking for trouble" when they saw the "new kid on the block" standing on the porch, a large snow shovel in hand. As Matt recalled decades later, "I never remember Jim wearing just casual clothes like blue jeans. On this day he was shoveling snow wearing a nice sweater and overcoat." This was a tempting target that a pack of young boys could not ignore. Quickly the gang rolled snowballs and pelted the dandy newcomer. Jim beat a hasty retreat inside, protesting loudly.[3]

What began as a friendly skirmish turned into warm and lasting relationships. Jim may not have catered to blue jeans and tennis shoes but he had no problem making friends and blending in with the neighborhood crew. Jim's sense of family would soon extend to this neighborhood and he discovered one of the delights that characterized his future life: loyal and lasting friendships.

At the same time that Jim was entering first grade, Bill was starting junior high. Slowly, Jim and Bill would become more distant as Bill moved into adolescence, separating himself further from home and seeking independence. However, JT became increasingly proud of Bill, who soon became a high school athlete, an excellent baseball player, and a top student. JT was open with his affirmation of Bill and saw him as an emerging bright star. As JT's focus and praise moved increasingly toward Bill, young Jim drew ever closer to his mother whose acceptance of him was clearly unconditional.[4]

Though supportive of the move to Jackson, Frances McAfee deeply missed her close-knit Hilliard clan in Chattanooga. One day she excitedly packed Jim's suitcase so he could accompany her on a grand adventure, a Greyhound bus trip back to Chattanooga to visit her family. They would stay with Frances's niece and closest friend, Anna Laura Hilliard Harding. It was Anna Laura, who had first introduced Frances to JT years before and set the course of Frances's life.

Arriving in Chattanooga, Jim trailed after his mother and innocently entered the familiarity of his Aunt Anna Laura's home. He was delighted to hear that he was still affectionately called "Buddy." He also met up again with his cousin, Diane Harding, a strong-willed ten-year-old who was three years older than Buddy and full of herself. She soon made it known that she was not happy to be babysitting Buddy and was particularly perturbed that Buddy would sleep in her bed while she was deported to the den couch. Later in the day, Frances and Anna Laura strolled to the corner store for groceries. Leaving the children inside the house for only a few minutes, the cat suddenly sprang on the mouse.

Turning to Buddy, Diane snapped, "I wish you were not here and I want you to go home!" Then she ran into her room, threw Buddy's clothes into his suitcase and marched him out onto the front porch. Handing Buddy his suitcase, Diane slipped inside the house, slammed the front door and locked it. Buddy was lost in the big wide world.

Assessing his situation, Buddy quietly sat down on the front porch and watched cars pass by. Within minutes Anna Laura and Frances returned to find Buddy waiting like a puppy on a chain. When his mother asked him what he was doing, he answered, "Diane told me to go home. But I waited. I knew I couldn't go home without you!"[5]

In McAfee family lore this is the story that best expresses Jim's relationship with his mother. She was his symbol of goodness and security, his reliable guide to find his way home when things grew difficult and he felt lost. Though distance would often separate them during adulthood, Jim always knew that "I can't go home without you."

Returning to Jackson, Jim expressed increasing interest in music, and he wanted to play the piano. Adjusting to a move and the costs of building a new house, JT was managing money closely. However, Frances had her small monthly allowance that JT doled out to her. From this allowance Frances was expected to run the home, which meant taking care of the children, buying gifts, purchasing clothes, and—if there was any money left over—providing for her own personal needs. Somehow Frances found a way to pay for Jim's piano lessons. Suddenly a life-long love of music was spawned. As Jim learned to read books, he also learned to read music. These two skills would open many positive and helpful doors in his future.[6]

One block from the McAfee house stood West Jackson Baptist Church. The McAfees' soon joined the fellowship of this vital congregation and the church became the hub of Jim's childhood and teenage social life. It cannot be underestimated how much this church family shaped Jim's emerging character, theology, ethics, and priorities.

The pastor at West Jackson Baptist Church was Dr. R.E. Guy. Dr. Guy was a conservative pastor of the old school Southern Baptist lineage. While a good and loving man, he was a staunch believer in the "thou shalt nots," one of which was not attending movies on Sunday afternoons.

One Sunday Jim talked his mother into taking him to an afternoon matinee at the local theater. Deciding to walk from their house into town, Frances McAfee was startled when a car pulled off the road in front of them and Dr. Guy stepped out to offer them a ride. Not wanting to rudely deny his offer, Frances and Jim hopped into the car only to hear the preacher ask, "Where can I take you, Frances?" Knowing that she could not possibly ask this pious man to drive them to the theater on the Sabbath and that all stores were closed on Sundays, Frances asked Dr. Guy to take them to a nearby friend's home. After Dr. Guy kindly dropped them off at a house two blocks from the theater, Frances and Jim quietly made their way back to their real destination. Jim learned from an early age that some Baptist beliefs were open to interpretation and that he did not have to obey every dictate of a preacher or denomination.

Later in Jim's teenage years, Dr. Guy would resign and a younger man, Dr. David Q. Byrd, was called to be the new pastor of West Jackson Baptist Church. Dr. Byrd was a likeable person and a New Testament scholar who had received his PhD from the respected Southern Baptist Theological Seminary in Louisville, Kentucky. Dr. Byrd was an able pastor and preacher and bequeathed to young Jim a respect for sound biblical study and the expectation of an educated and professional clergy. Dr. Byrd was also open-minded and not overly conservative. As an adult, Jim wanted his pastor to be as equally trained and competent as his physician, attorney, or accountant. He also desired a pastor who was open-minded, progressive, and had a sense of humor. Dr. Byrd set a high standard that Jim respected.

However, the staff member at West Jackson Baptist Church who best served as a mentor for Jim was Rev. H. Lowrey Haynie, the minister of music. Lowrey Haynie was not your typical church musician. He studied music and education at Memphis State University and received a master's degree in music education from George Peabody College, now merged with Vanderbilt University in Nashville, Tennessee. During World War II, Rev. Haynie was a

Marine in the Pacific Campaign and directed a divisional band. As a result, Haynie achieved excellence in church music programs and expected his children and youth choirs to snap to attention. He created an *esprit de corps* that unified young people and drew them closer together through collaborative musical effort. Teenagers loved and respected Haynie, and Jim was no exception.

Rev. Haynie symbolized the importance of mutual commitment by requiring that his youth choirs have a dress code when they performed. As young boys moved toward their teenage years they were required to wear a white shirt and a uniform tie when they sang in worship or in concert. One day Jim neglected dress code and appeared in a flashy tie of his own choosing. Jim was soon sitting alone on the front row, watching the choir sing without him. It was a lesson he never forgot. Rev. Haynie was a welcoming friend, a worthy model, and an exacting mentor for a growing child seeking male affirmation and blessing.[7]

Music would remain a life-long love of Jim McAfee's. His mother often said that she could tell what kind of mood Jim was in by the way he played the piano. When he was down, he would play the blues. And when he was up, jazz could erupt in the living room. Music was a close companion that would walk with Jim down every pathway of his life. This love began with his mother's early encouragement to play the piano and read music. This same love of music would draw him to his future wife.[8]

As a child, Jim was mesmerized by cars. His childhood buddy, Hampton ("Hamp") Williams, Jr., also loved cars, and the little boys would sit on the ridge of Jim's front yard engaged in fierce competition. Their game revolved around who could most quickly and most accurately identify the model and production date of each automobile that passed by. They spent hours in this pursuit and dreamed of the cars they would drive when they grew up.

However, to obtain a car, Jim realized at an early age that he would need to find a job and save his money. This desire became a childhood goal and ushered in perhaps the most dominant passion, gift, and ability of Jim's personhood: the desire to work hard and diligently toward clearly defined goals. Jim's greatest talent was a natural inclination for industry, planning, and focused attention.[9]

Jim's first childhood employment was with a regional newspaper company, *The Memphis Commercial Appeal.* As an eleven-year-old still in elementary school, Jim was hired to go house-to-house in nearby neighborhoods collecting the monthly billings for the newspaper. He received a small commission from his collections and learned to be honest, reliable, and accurate when dealing with money.[10]

This job also prompted Jim to develop public relations skills long before he had heard this term. Many of the accounts that he managed were delinquent. This was a delicate subject. Jim had the childlike ability not to offend people who were behind on their payments and yet the maturity to knock on a door and converse politely with adults of all natures and personalities. Jim enjoyed his work and was good at it.

While collecting subscription fees, Jim developed a method of remembering people that he would use all of his life. When Jim met a new customer, he quietly created a unique nickname for this person that would characterize them and lodge in his memory. Most of Jim's friends were also given special names. Sometimes you might not understand why Jim gave you your new name. But Jim always had a reason. And he seldom forgot.[11]

Several times when Jim received his monthly salary based on his commissions, he noted that the amount that he had been paid did not equal his own calculations. Jim found the courage to politely ask his manager to recalculate his earnings. Each time Jim's calculations proved to be correct. Jim learned in this process to always "keep an eye on the ledger book." Even in his later years when Jim was eating in a favorite restaurant, he would always carefully scrutinize the bill before paying the charge. This was not an issue of trust for Jim. Rather it was business ethics and healthy frugality.[12]

When Jim turned thirteen he resigned from *The Memphis Commercial Appeal* and accepted a paper route with the local *Jackson Sun.* This was a demanding job. Seven days a week, rain or shine, Jim rose at dawn to ride his bike to the paper distribution center. He would roll his papers and fasten them with a rubber band. He then stuffed the papers into his pouch and pedaled off into a fresh new morning.

Jim rode through all types of neighborhoods: the rich and the poor, middle class and shanty towns, bootleggers and bars, and witnessed the rigid segregation of black and white America in the 1950s. This broadening of his social perspective created early opinions of what kind of world he aspired to live in. As he rushed to get home for breakfast and dress for school, he dreamed of his future and how he might contribute to society. Jim was emerging from the shelter of his childhood confines and learning lessons that cannot be taught in a classroom.

Jim was also accepting increased responsibility. The *Jackson Sun* paid their paper route boys based on seniority and length of tenure. Their policy stated that if a paper was not delivered promptly and correctly, you were "busted down" to the lowest pay rank. Jim was never busted. He was gaining insight into competition, customer service, and reliability.[13]

While in elementary school, Jim's mother often had sick spells. Jim's close childhood friend Hamp Williams recalls that he would often go to Jim's house to play and they would build plastic models of cars or work on Jim's Lionel electric train in an unfinished attic room. However, on the days that Mrs. McAfee was having headaches, the noise of the train and the sound of their feet on the attic floor were more than Mrs. McAfee could bear. Jim and Hamp would go outside or to Hamp's house to play and let her rest without the disturbance that young boys make.[14]

Though it was kept quiet and diffused, there was tension building at home. JT, though a good and faithful man, was also strict, exacting, and hard to live with. His Scottish frugality and childhood scars often emerged over issues of money and expenditure. Bill learned to escape this tension through his involvement in high school sports and academics, and Jim increasingly lost himself in work and church activities. But Mrs. McAfee was often the buffer and the quiet target of JT's intensity. In an era when most mothers did not work outside the home, her limited education also restricted her professional opportunities. Though active in church work, she often felt trapped at home. Her headaches and sensitive health were likely caused by multiple factors, but one of the overriding factors was coping with JT's dominant personality.

As Jim approached junior high and high school, he was quite aware of this unhealthy dynamic at home and was determined to support and protect his mother. Just as she was Jim's champion, so was Jim her defender and advocate. This dynamic would be life-long.[15]

As Jim completed elementary and junior high school and entered adolescence, he was satisfied to stay in the middle of the pack academically and not follow his older brother on to the baseball and football fields. However, he had clearly identified himself as a child with an intense work ethic, a desire to find personal freedom through making his own money, a longing for friendship, a passion for music, and an increasing devotion to Christian faith.

Chapter 4

High School Years, 1953–1957

When fourteen-year-old Jim entered Jackson High School in 1953, the United States was mired in the Korean War but still energized by the strength of a post-World War II economy. Mandated racial integration of public schools had not begun and the Civil Rights Movement was just simmering. Jackson High School was the only "white" high school in Jackson, Tennessee, a city with a population in 1950 of 30,200. Jackson was the epitome of an old county-seat Southern town, rooted in brick-and-ivy tradition but also enriched by the stimulating presence of Union University, a small Southern Baptist school with 1,000 undergraduate students.[1]

As Jim began his first day as a freshman, he was physically a late bloomer. Not yet having hit his growth spurt, he was short, a bit pudgy, still imbued with the cherubic "Buddy" look, and had not a whisker on his chin. Unlike his strapping brother Bill, who was now at Union University, Jim was not an honor student or a first-rate athlete. Rather, he wore glasses, toted a leather trombone case to band practice, and longed for the day he could apply for his driver's license.[2]

That day finally came, and a new sense of liberation was at hand. Jim had saved his newspaper money to buy a car, and he knew exactly what he intended to purchase. A neighbor had a 1940 Ford stored up on blocks in his garage. The four-door Ford was shiny black and in mint condition. Jim asked his father to see if the neighbor would be willing to sell the car. A price of $75 was negotiated, and Jim coughed up his hard-earned cash. In the exuberant words of Jim's high school buddy, Bobby Haynie, "We were now all free!!!"[3]

And free they were. The Ford was huge, with wide running boards and an interior so large it seemed it could hold a marching band. One night the boys made bets as to how many people could fit in the car. They removed the seats and Jim used a cinder block as a driver's seat. Cramming as many friends as they could into the Ford, Jim carefully drove around the block. The head count is now forgotten, but the memory is vivid for the seventy-year-olds who still recall that eventful moment.[4]

Shortly after buying the car, Jim and Matt Tomlin were driving downtown. The engine began to smoke and burst into flame. Passing directly in front of the fire station, Jim wheeled in, screeching brakes in front of the parked fire engine and blowing his horn. Within seconds, the fire was doused and Jim's lifetime investment was saved.[5]

Because Jim was the first of his friends to own a car, he gained a new sense of pride and notoriety. As Bobby Haynie recalled, "We were all jealous of him!" But Jim's true connection with people was not his driver's license but his charismatic personality—he could make friends with an oak stump.[6]

Jim's closest friends were Matt Tomlin, Hamp Williams, and Bobby Haynie. Matt, Bobby, and Jim all attended West Jackson Baptist Church. Hamp was a Methodist and did not quite understand his friends' conservative Baptist theology, with its strict doctrine of "don't drink, smoke, or chew and don't go with girls that do!" The boys went to Sunday school together, participated in a Baptist boys' organization called *Royal Ambassadors*, and sang next to each other in youth choir. During the school week, they played instruments in the high school band at football games and the pep band at basketball games. Because Jim played a mean and resonant trombone, he was soon stuck with the nickname, "The Slide." Church and school were the foundations of their teenage years.[7]

The early 1950s was also a treasured time when neighborhood families knew each other and there was close community. Bobby Haynie's high school sweetheart (and future wife) was Becky Maness. Becky's father, Ellis Maness, was the contractor who built JT McAfee's house. The McAfee and Maness families lived in the same neighborhood, and Mr. Maness had the distinction of buying the first television set within that community. On summer nights, Mr. Maness would often open his large living room window and position this massive monstrosity of technological curiosity so that the neighbors would see the bright black-and-white screen from across the yard. Like moths drawn by the light, the neighbors would leave their front porches and bring lawn chairs over to watch the wonder of television in the Maness front yard. Sitting outside or laying on blankets, they ate peanuts, drank Coca-Colas, and laughed themselves silly amidst the antics of *Amos and Andy, I Love Lucy,* and *The Jackie Gleason Show*. This was a special moment in time, a snapshot of *Americana.*[8]

Practical jokes were also part of Jim's high-school life. One day Matt Tomlin and Jim drove into the country to go fishing. Catching several nice bass and a few large catfish, they put the fish in a metal cooler of water to keep them alive until they could go home and clean them. As they drove back into town that evening—fish still captive in the trunk—they drove past West Jackson Baptist Church and Jim had a moment of inspiration. Knowing that the next day there would be a baptism and that the baptistery was now full of water, he suddenly made a sharp turn into the church parking lot. Finding a way into the darkened sanctuary, the boys placed their catch of fish into the four-foot-deep baptismal pool and quietly snuck away.

The next morning during Sunday school, things "broke loose" in the Baptist church. A red-faced deacon sailed into the high-school boys' class demanding to know who had put the fish in the baptistery. Jim and Matt confessed and were soon trying to catch the fish with a dip net before the worship service started. Jesus' admonition to be "fishers of men" never had the same meaning to either boy again.[9]

Jim also developed one or two bad habits at church that would plague him for many years. Whether Jim smoked his first cigarette on church premises is doubtful, but one summer he attended a Royal Ambassador Camp and yielded to temptation. Boys being boys, Jim and his buddies were soon smoking cigarettes in the woods or in the dormitory bathrooms by open windows late at night. Following the telltale trace of tobacco smoke, the adult counselors soon caught their prey and brought them to justice. Each was duly convicted of sin, sought repentance, and pledged never to smoke again.

However, this was one promise that Jim could not keep. He truly loved his Winston cigarettes and would smoke a pack a day for many years. The rich fragrance and chemical allure brought a sense of comfort and calm to an intense and over-committed teenager. In a day when cigarettes were still issued to every military recruit, they were a sign of manhood and an acceptable way to reduce stress.[10]

As Jim entered high school, his brother, Bill, had already left home and moved on to Union University. Now, Jim had the house to himself. During college, Bill felt a *calling* to become a Baptist minister. This pleased both JT and Frances, and they supported his decision. When Bill graduated from Union University, he enrolled at the Southern Baptist Theological Seminary in Louisville, Kentucky. However, within a year, Bill realized that though he wanted to minister to the needs of people, he was better suited to be a physician than a pastor. JT agreed to help him financially as he transferred to the University of Tennessee College of Medicine in Memphis. Jim looked on from afar and began to ponder what vocation he might follow in his future.

As Jim continued through high school, he dated many different girls. Jim and Matt Tomlin often double-dated. While Baptist youth were encouraged not to dance due to the lust and sexual ardor that might be stirred while on the dance floor, more sedate movies and trips to the drive-in theater were not off limits, as long as they were not attended on Sundays. Occasionally driving eighty miles to the big-city sights of Memphis enlivened a boring weekend. But more frequently, get-togethers after basketball games, band trips to out-of-town football games, sweetheart banquets at the church on Valentine's Day, or just cruising the Jackson Dairy Queen comprised the social life of Jackson High School students.

Jim became a teenager during the birth of the American rock 'n' roll era. Elvis Presley was playing his guitar, shaking his pelvis, and scandalizing the Southern Baptists' sense of propriety in the Southland. Elvis's international stage was centered in nearby Memphis, Tennessee; however, Jim never grew his hair long, wore a ducktail flip, squeezed himself into tight Levis, or wore black penny loafers with white crew socks. Jim was not the Bill Haley, Jimmy Dean, or Buddy Holly type. He remained predictably traditional, and more of a Glenn Miller or Tommy Dorsey "Big-Band-Sound" man. But one day he had his inevitable confrontation with the Jackson version of the black-leather rock and roll "Fonzie."

This older boy was a bully. Jimmy Dean to the core, he could not afford a true macho motorcycle, but he did own a souped-up motor scooter. "The Fonzie" had learned to do impressive wheel-stands in the high school parking lot with this low-powered steed and relished making a lot of noise with custom-made exhaust pipes. He saw himself as a Marlon Brando bad boy with Steve McQueen machismo.

One day, as Jim stepped out of the door of the band room and onto the high school parking lot, the bully was holding court with several girls. Seeing Jim walking toward his Ford, he shot toward him on his motor scooter as if to run him over. Jim stopped, stunned, and simply faced him. Flustered, the bully revved his engine and began to make short lunges toward him. Jim quickly side-stepped and suddenly watched his own fist shoot forward in slow motion and shatter the

Fonzie's windshield. The tough kid on the motorcycle melted. Embarrassed and unmasked, he turned and sped away, cursing a blue streak.

In that moment Jim left "Buddy" behind and found a steel glint in his eyes that would often be seen as he faced adversity in the future. Jim never forsook amiability, friendship, and politeness, but courage and toughness had also found their place within the repertoire of his varied personality. Jim learned quiet fortitude in high school.[11]

Much harder than standing up to the bully at high school, however, was dealing with his father at home. JT McAfee was neither a bad man nor an unkind person. He was amiable, provided for his family, and loved both his sons. He was respected in the community, in his church, and successful in his work. Indeed, Jim's close friend, Matt Tomlin, does not remember Jim being estranged from his father or JT being "unpleasant."[12]

Similarly, Hamp Williams reflected that he truly liked Jim's father but that he did detect a "certain tension in the family." And Bobby Haynie recalled those teenage days sixty years later and simply said, "Jim's Dad was very strict, but I could tell that Mr. McAfee truly cared for Jim. His Dad was a good guy and kids looked up to him. He liked to kid around with us kids. I wouldn't say anything negative about Mr. McAfee, but looking back, I can see a tension."[13]

What was this "tension" about? The primary issue was the compromised ability of a loving father to give his clear *blessing* to his younger son. It is important to take a moment to ask: How is this issue of blessing best defined and understood?

The concept of "blessing" emanates from both Judaism and Christianity. In an ancient Hebrew society, it was important for a Jewish father to give a son his personal blessing before the father died. Though a blessing included the giving of inheritance, it meant far more than money and possessions. At its deepest level the blessing was a rite of passage that made clear a father's love, acceptance, and praise of his son. The Hebrew root word that is translated as *blessing* means *to speak well of* or *to praise*. The opposite of to bless is to curse. To adequately bless your child is to consistently communicate over the course of a lifetime the message: I love you for who you are. I accept you as you are. And though I may not agree with you at all times–or condone all of your behavior and decisions—I believe and trust you.

A primal scene of a father bestowing his blessing is found in Genesis 27:1–40 when a blind and ailing Isaac gives his blessing to his younger son, Jacob, but inadvertently withholds the blessing from his older son, Esau. A second scene of giving blessing is found in Jesus' parable of the prodigal son depicted in Luke 15:15–32. In both of these ancient stories there are two sets of competitive and contrasting brothers who are earnestly seeking to be blessed by their father. In each instance one son finds a way to receive the blessing but the second son never connects to the gift of his father's blessing.

When ancient Isaac placed his hands of blessing upon Jacob's head, he symbolically said, You are pleasing to me. I speak well of you. You are worthy of my trust, my lineage, my love, the profit of my lifetime. I am proud of you.

In Jesus' parable, when a grieving and patient father sees his hard-headed and defiant youngest son staggering home from a far-off land, mere words will not express his blessing. He runs to greet him and embraces him. Inviting him into the family house, he drapes a robe of royalty around his dirty shoulders, puts a family signet ring on his finger, and places new shoes on his bare feet. He exults, "You can never be my servant, you can only be the one thing you truly are—my son!"

Even Jesus received the blessing of his Heavenly Father when he emerged out of the baptismal waters of the River Jordan and heard words resonate within his heart: "This is my beloved son *in whom I am well pleased*!"

And so, scenes such as these were acted out in the McAfee house, perhaps rumbling over the course of many intertwined generations. There were two brothers: Bill, named for his grandfather, and Jim, named for his father. Though both Bill and Jim struggled with their relationship with their father—and both felt to varying degrees estranged from him—it seems that JT was able to demonstrate openly his pride in Bill. The older son may have rebelled against JT's intensity, strict discipline, and tight-fistedness, but JT let it be known that he was proud of Bill's athletic achievement, academic prowess, and later his professional role as a medical doctor. He noticeably beamed as Bill walked across the stage of life. JT was extremely pleased.

But this was not true for Jim. Though equally as focused and industrious as his older brother, Jim did not seek the outward symbols of making the honor roll or earning a letterman jacket. Jim's father was not musical and could not appreciate playing an instrument or marching in the band. Nor did it seem that Jim was beginning to direct his interest toward acclaimed professions such as medicine or law or divinity. Rather, Jim revealed an emerging interest in more mundane business pursuits. Realizing at an early age this lack of connection with his father and feeling the absence of any real approval, Jim distanced himself and, as we have seen, turned to his mother for blessing.

Ironically, even though Jim bore the name James Thomas McAfee, Jr., his father seldom beamed and brightened when Jim walked across the stage of his adolescent life. Rather than feel the warmth of the paternal blessing, Jim often detected the whisper of a silent curse, "I'm afraid you will not amount to much."[14] Jim was determined to dispel the curse and prove his father wrong.

Chapter 5

College Years, 1957–1961

The high school years passed quickly enough, and Jim soon graduated from Jackson High in May 1957. This was the beginning of an era in American history characterized by radical change and increasing anxiety. When high school classes began the next fall in nearby Little Rock, Arkansas, President Eisenhower was forced to order elements of the elite 101st Airborne division to go to Little Rock Central High School and enforce the Supreme Court decision to integrate public schools. The racial violence and ugliness of this moment sent tremors through Jim's community two hundred miles away.

Internationally, American involvement in a civil war in Vietnam was escalating, fueled by a fear that the combined communist powers of the USSR and China intended to take over the world. This "Red scare" intensified when Russia vaulted ahead in the space race with their successful launching of Sputnik in 1957, the first human made object to orbit the earth. Many feared that a third world war was looming.[1]

In the midst of such transition, many things in Jim's life remained the same. Rather than enter a university in another city or state, Jim enrolled at Union University, located less than two miles from his childhood home in Jackson. He continued to attend West Jackson Baptist Church, and his best friends Matt Tomlin and Bobby Haynie also enrolled at Union University. High school and college merged smoothly together.

As Jim concluded high school, his older brother, Bill, had left Southern Baptist Theological Seminary to enter medical school. Bill was fulfilling his father's early dream of becoming a physician. Proud

Frances Zoe Hilliard McAfee, 1932.

Jim McAfee, 1940.

Jim McAfeee, age two.

Bill McAfee, Frances McAfee, Jim McAfee, 1944 Chattanooga, TN.

Jim McAfee, age three.

Frances Zoe Hilliard McAfee and Jim McAfee, 1944.

Jim McAfee, age ten.

Jim McAfee, Age twelve.

Jim McAfee, age fifteen.

Jim McAfee's senior picture, 1957, Jackson High School, Jackson, TN.

Jim McAfee's 1960 SAE fraternity picture, Union University, Jackson, TN.

Jim McAfee and Carolyn Townsend McAfee at their wedding,
September 1, 1962, First Baptist Church, Parsons, TN.

Jim and Carolyn's first house, Manchester, TN.

John W. Harton Memorial Hospital, 1968, Tullahoma, TN.

Proud parents, 1968.

Carolyn McAfee, Tom McAfee, and Jim McAfee, Christmas 1969, Jackson, TN.

Jim McAfee, Tom McAfee, and J. T. McAfee,
Christmas 1969, Jackson, TN.

Cathy McAfee Maiocco, Tom McAfee, Bob McAfee, J. T. McAfee, Paul McAfee, Carolyn McAfee, Frances McAfee, and Nancy McAfee at the McAfee Christmas dinner, 1969, Jackson, TN.

Frances McAfee, Jim McAfee, Tom McAfee, and J. T. McAfee, 1969 Huntsville, AL.

Jim McAfee and Tom McAfee, 1979, Seabrook Island, SC.

J. T. McAfee, Jim McAfee, and Tom McAfee
at Jim's fortieth birthday, 1979, Atlanta, GA.

Tom McAfee and Jim McAfee, 1982, Macon, GA. "Get to work!"

Tom McAfee and Jim McAfee, 1984, Macon, GA.
"Can't you clean the pool any faster?"

Carolyn McAfee, Jim McAfee, and Tom McAfee at the dedication of the Carolyn Townsend McAfee Organ, 1990, Union University, Jackson, TN.

Jim McAfee, Tom McAfee, Carolyn McAfee, Nancy McAfee, Bill McAfee, Cathy Maiocco, and J. T. McAfee at the dedication of the Frances Zoe Hilliard McAfee Commons, 1990, Union University, Jackson, TN.

Back row: C. D. Hilliard, Jerri Hilliard, Sophia Townsend, Tom McAfee, Jim McAfee, and Carolyn McAfee. Front row: Raymond Townsend and J. T. McAfee. The group celebrates Jim receiving an honorary doctor of Laws from Union University, 1994.

Jim McAfee, bicycling on Isle of Colonsay, Scotland, 1994.

Jim McAfee and Carolyn McAfee
at Kiloran Bay, Isle of Colonsay, Scotland, 1999.

Jim McAfee and Carolyn McAfee
at the Miller-Howe House, Windermere, England, 1998.

Tom McAfee and Jim McAfee
at the Miller-Howe House, Lake Windermere, England, 1998.

Jim McAfee at the MacPhie Standing Stone,
Isle of Colonsay, Scotland, 1995.

Jim McAfee at the Kildrummy Castle gardens, Scotland, 2002.

Jim McAfee in Scotland.

Tom McAfee and Jim McAfee enjoying azaleas at the Atlanta house, 1995.

Carolyn McAfee and Jim McAfee; 1990.

Jim McAfee, Ponkey VII; celebrating Jim's birthday at Seabrook Island, SC.

Jim McAfee, Ponkey VI; enjoying the newspaper.

Jim McAfee "having a conversation with Black Jack and enjoying the view." Seabrook Island, SC.

Jim McAfee, Christmas 2002, Seabrook Island, SC.

Jim McAfee, Peggy Pillow, and Nathan Pillow, June 1995.

Jim McAfee honors Tullahoma, TN doctors and spouses,
2002, Tullahoma, TN.

Diane Harding Hill and Jim McAfee reminisce about the old days.

Jim McAfee entertains the Hilliard family: Anna Laura Harding, Dianne Hill, and Sara Ruth Hilliard, 1993, Atlanta, GA.

Jim McAfee and Carolyn McAfee, Big Canoe, GA.

Jim McAfee relaxes to music.

Jim McAfee playing his Ibach piano.

Carolyn McAfee and Jim McAfee
in the Rainbow Room, 1994, New York, NY.

Raymond Townsend, Sophia Townsend, Carolyn McAfee, and Tom McAfee, Christmas 1994, Atlanta, GA.

Jim McAfee, Jim Dahr, and Wayne McAlister perform at the Charter Medical Talent Show, Hamilton, Bermuda.

Jackson High School Class of 1957 reunion, Bob Hundley (Jim's seventh grade teacher) Mary Ruth Hundley, and Jim McAfee.

1994 Hallmark Healthcare directors: (front) Roland A. Maxwell, James T. McAfee, Jr., and Robert Thornton, as well as (back) James E. Martin, Kay W. Slayden, and Randy Seckman.

Jim McAfee and Bob Thornton celebrate the sale of Hallmark Healthcare, 1994, Atlanta, GA.

of Bill's ambition and academic achievement, JT enthusiastically agreed to help Bill pay tuition for medical school. Quietly watching JT loosen the purse strings, Jim decided that he would pay his own way through college. This was a matter of pride as well as necessity for Jim. He wanted the independence that comes with financial self-reliance.

To accomplish his goal, Jim began a significant trend of working two or three part-time jobs simultaneously. He first applied to be a salesman at J. C. Penney Co. Jim soon realized that he had a gift for business, and he often accumulated more sales by the end of the week than many full-time employees. He was given the nickname "Speedy" for his ability to hustle and close a deal.

But more than being competitive and gifted, Jim was also demonstrating a genuine attitude of care and concern for others. On several occasions, Jim noticed that one of the sales staff was having a bad month and was lagging behind in their sales commissions. Most of these people were married with families to support. Jim frequently made a sale, but placed another salesman's name and number on the transaction so that the commission would be credited to their account. It was his quiet way of helping out.[2]

Jim also worked part-time for Tigrett Industries and came to know his first prominent business entrepreneur. The Tigretts were a leading family in Jackson and had amassed wealth during the railroad boom. John Burton Tigrett multiplied the wealth of the railroad years through assorted business ventures, such as creating some of the first plastic toys that were mechanical in nature. Paying $800 for the patent for *Glub-Glub the Duck,* a toy that bobs and appears to guzzle water, Tigrett soon sold 22 million of these plastic wonders and made a fortune. Later, having seen his son cut himself on a wooden playpen, John Tigrett invented a safer playpen constructed of plastic mesh that was soon sold to major chains such as Sears and Roebuck, where millions of these cribs were sold around the world.[3]

Born in 1913, John Tigrett, had lived briefly in an orphanage as a child until taken in by his wealthy uncle, Isaac Tigrett, the railroad baron of Jackson, Tennessee. John later gave Isaac credit for teaching him the importance of being financially independent. In later life, John would say, "I've never depended on anyone for a salary, and that independence has proven invaluable over the years."[4]

As young Jim McAfee dreamed about college and his future, he watched thousands of *Glub-Glub the Ducks* bob their way down the assembly line. He pondered on John Tigrett's striving for financial independence through entrepreneurial ventures. And so, Jim, too, came to believe that work is not something to be endured, but something to be enjoyed; that a business venture is indeed a source of great challenge, pleasure, and joy. And above all, Jim embraced what he already knew to be true—that competitive business pursuits are just as enticing and challenging as success on a football field or a baseball diamond. A personal dream of financial independence bred from business savvy grew clearer.

Another aspect of Jim's work at Tigrett Industries involved working in their personnel department. The seasonal aspects of toy production caused the industry to have a long list of part-time employees who were called in to work only when production increased during busy times such as Christmas or Easter. These part-time employees were also summoned to fill in when a full-time employee was ill or absent. It was Jim's job to call these part-time employees and ask them to come to work.

Jim soon learned that many people were out of work, not because of laziness, but rather because of adverse and unique conditions. When Jim called these men and women and asked them to report to work on the assembly line, he often heard the joy in their voices as they grasped an opportunity to make extra money to feed their children or pay their electricity bill. This experience gave to Jim empathy and concern for minimum-wage employees that would later shape his thoughts and attitude as a business executive.

Often, when Jim was not needed at the toy factory, he was asked to be a chauffeur for the Tigrett children, driving them to their various activities. This personal knowledge and bond with the family also enabled Jim to understand that successful entrepreneurs are "real-live people" who eat, sleep, and work like everyone else. These were important insights for an emerging young adult with unusually sharp business acumen. This experience imbued Jim with ambition and hope.[5]

When there were any hours left over in a day, Jim also worked for Perel and Lowenstein Credit Jewelry Store on East Main Street. Because much of their merchandise was bought on credit, there was a need for someone to collect bad debts and make repossessions. Jim was sometimes given this onerous task.

Once, Jim was sent to an address to repossess a pair of eyeglasses from a woman who had not made payments. Jim knocked on her door and an impoverished elderly African-American lady greeted him politely and asked him in. As Jim looked around at her surroundings, he knew that this lady had no money to spare. Yet without her glasses she was legally blind. Rather than repossess the glasses, Jim departed determined that he would negotiate an equitable resolution for her. Finding the courage to address the owners of the jewelry store, they all quickly agreed that whatever terms this woman needed could be arranged and that under no circumstances would her glasses be taken away from her.

Jim was learning about business ethics. Most specifically, he intuitively knew that empathy and compassion, both of which are at the heart of the teachings of Hebrew and Christian scripture, must be part of all endeavors. The long hours of sitting in wooden pews at West Jackson Baptist Church were paying off. Good business could be based on Christ-like ethics and a desire to share with the poor, the needy, and the oppressed. Through his diverse work Jim was receiving more than a college education even before he attended his first class at Union University.

When all of his day jobs were juggled, balanced, and in order, Jim also worked at night at a small local motel, The Holiday Courts. The motel was owned by Jim's neighbor and family friend Ellis Maness, who had helped the McAfees build their home. A member of Jim's church, Mr. Maness was not well educated, but had become a local business success through hard work and smart business investments. Above all, he loved teenagers and was personally involved in their activities. Mr. Maness had encouraged Jim, laughed at his antics, and now entrusted Jim to be a night auditor and bookkeeper for his motel. Such trust from a true mentor helped Jim to believe in himself and motivated him to learn basic principles of accounting. There is nothing like a mentor's trust to encourage a young adult to do well.

When the fall semester finally started in 1957, Jim was caught up in the mad rush of freshman activity. He lived at home in order to save money, but he also decided to rush a fraternity and was soon initiated into Sigma Alpha Epsilon (SAE). This fraternity, founded in 1856 at his maternal grandfather's alma mater, the University of Alabama, was the first national fraternity to be founded in the Antebellum South. The SAE brothers were known as a well-dressed, well-heeled, traditional, and hard-partying group of young men. They had their share of fun and shenanigans and, in Jim's estimation, were a "great bunch of guys."

Fraternity life played a significant role in Jim's college experience. The fraternity house became his base of operations on the Union University campus, and his fraternity brothers became his closest friends. Frequently when he did not want to go home, he would stay overnight at the fraternity house, engrossed in intense conversation and loving the fun-filled life-style. His fraternity dues were $10 per month.

One of Jim's fraternity brothers was Nathan Pillow, a Tennessee boy who had wandered far away to Baylor University in Waco, Texas, and who had recently decided to move back closer to home and attend Union University. Nathan was a Bible-toting "preacher boy" who could also keep pace with his fraternity brothers. Filled with an outgoing personality and a love for life, Nathan was someone that Jim respected and yet could enjoy fun times. These Baptist boys made an interesting duo and shared in much mischief together.

One night while hanging out at the fraternity house, Nathan prodded Jim into raiding the underwear drawer of the most rotund freshman member of the fraternity. The prank soon got out of hand, and another brother made the underwear "permanently disappear." When the young freshman took a shower and dressed for class the next morning, he found himself in an embarrassing predicament—much too large and timid to borrow underwear from someone else. When the laughter finally subsided, Jim felt badly about the situation and quickly drove to J. C. Penney Co. to buy the boy new underwear. Sneaking his purchase back into the fraternity house, the underwear miraculously reappeared.[6]

At the same time that Nathan and Jim were learning about fraternity life, Nathan was leading youth revivals around western Tennessee. Though Jim did not see himself as a "preacher boy," Nathan occasionally talked Jim into leading music at his revival services. Fraternities and revival tents merged together at Baptist universities in the 1950s.

As Jim grew closer to his new college friends, he developed a reputation for being present in times of trouble. One of his SAE brothers was particularly struggling personally and academically. His problem was not lack of ability but rather blatant immaturity. By the end of his first semester he was on academic probation and had risen to the top of Dean F.E. Wright's "blacklist." Finally, after one weekend of exceptional misbehavior, this young man was summoned to Dean Wright's office and expelled from Union University.

Concerned about his fraternity brother's welfare and future, Jim engaged his courage and made an appointment to talk with Dr. Wright. As he entered the dean's office his knees were knocking. However, he soon developed a rapport with the good-natured dean and convinced him to change his ruling from suspension to probation. As a result, when Jim's friend returned for his second semester, he was a changed man. He attended class under the watchful scrutiny of his fraternity brothers and his grades and behavior soon improved.

Several years later when Jim was an upperclassman, he had the opportunity to return the favor to Dean Wright when Dr. Wright became critically ill with an extended illness. It became apparent that Dr. Wright's health insurance would not adequately cover his medical costs and he faced a personal financial crisis. Jim was concerned and led a campaign to raise funds, not only on campus but also throughout the city of Jackson. Citizens of Jackson as well as students and faculty responded, and Dean Wright's medical bills were paid. A theme was emerging in Jim's life of becoming a man who would not desert a friend in times of trouble or even poor judgment. Jim was faithful and devoted. As Jim's fraternity brother Nathan Pillow would comment years later, "One of Jim's strongest traits was standing by you."[7]

As Jim continued into his freshman year at Union, his love of music grew and he soon joined the University Choir and the stage band—an instrumental ensemble that played at basketball games and other events. "The Slide" was back in action playing his trombone and loving the big band sound.

At this time, Jim also noticed a pretty, petite young woman who was also a freshman and who played the alto saxophone in the band. He learned that she was a music major studying organ performance. Her name was Carolyn Townsend and she was from Parsons,

Tennessee, forty-five miles east of Jackson. Jim was instantly attracted and decided to ask her for a date at the first opportunity.

Carolyn, too, had noticed Jim during freshman orientation in Powell Chapel. She remembered him as being funny and a tease. However, it was not love at first sight. Carolyn was smitten by the charms of another young man, and when Jim asked her to go with him to a Training Union social at West Jackson Baptist Church, she found an excuse to decline. Being turned down by your first college crush is a part of the experience of many freshmen boys. Though nursing wounded pride, Jim soon snapped back and chased other women. But he never took his eyes off Carolyn Townsend. And he never forgot that she sidestepped his first invitation.[8]

At the same time that Jim began college classes, in the fall of 1957, a fresh, new college professor who had recently graduated from New Orleans Baptist Theological Seminary stepped foot on the Union campus. His name was Dr. Hyran Barefoot, and his doctorate was in New Testament and Greek. A native of Mantee, Mississippi, Dr. Barefoot was bright, energetic, progressive, and engaging with students. Through Dr. Barefoot and other members of the religion faculty, Jim McAfee soon found that his required Bible classes were some of the most interesting courses in the undergraduate curriculum. Suddenly Jim was being challenged to move beyond a "Sunday School mentality" and to critically engage how the Bible was written, to assess the teachings of Jesus of Nazareth, and to critique the epistles of the Apostle Paul. One of the greatest academic gifts that Jim received at Union University was to meet inspiring religion professors such as Hyran Barefoot who encouraged him to think, to question, and to discern what he really believed. This experience made Jim greatly appreciate the importance of Baptist higher education and to value theological exploration, not only for the clergy, but also for the laity. This realization would shape Jim's future path and his commitment to Christian education.[9]

Though intellectually curious, intelligent and motivated, Jim did not aspire to make his mark as an outstanding student or honor graduate within his class. What he did determine is that he would work to squeeze every drop of vitality and energy out of each day of his life. Soon he decided to be a business major and not to wait until graduation to engage in making money. He would pursue this goal immediately.

While in college Jim began investing in the stock market with what little cash he had left after paying his monthly expenses. Learning about stocks, bonds, and commodities was an education that was real and stimulating. No grades were given for this endeavor, but Jim did not need to be graded to know that successful business ventures were of vital importance. As Nathan Pillow would later say of his classmate, "Mac was intense and focused in college. He took his various jobs seriously, his studies seriously, and particularly focused on business studies at Union.... There was not a lazy bone in Mac's body. He was a hustler. He played the stock market back then and had the unique ability to see something when it was down, buy it, and make it successful."[10]

Nathan also recalled when Jim discovered that the financial markets can "bite you!" Jim was watching the commodities market and noted that the price of eggs was dropping. When Jim felt that the price had reached its lowest ebb, he purchased hundreds of eggs. He was mistaken and soon the bottom really dropped out of the egg market. Jim received an urgent call from his broker saying, "Where do you want your eggs delivered, Mr. McAfee?"

Nathan Pillow remembers that this "scared Jim to death." Suddenly the SAE house was filled with stacks of cartons of eggs that were perishable. Jim rallied the troops, and he and his friend James "Cotton" Couch canvassed the countryside selling eggs for bargain prices at every country store and crossroads town they could find in western Tennessee. Jim managed to save his investment, but it took a lot of work and time away from studying to come out even. Jim did not buy any more eggs—and he never forgot the lesson.[11]

As Jim rose out of the freshman ranks and continued through college, he gained a reputation for being a go-to and get-it-fixed kind of guy, both within his fraternity and on the wider campus. Once, the brothers of Sigma Alpha Epsilon found themselves in a serious financial crisis and were in danger of having their fraternity house repossessed by the bank. Jim was elected treasurer and tasked with solving the problem. Jim put on his best suit, starched shirt and tie, and went to talk with the bank officers. Not wanting to shut down a fraternity or tamper with Union University, a plan for restoring order was soon worked out and terms agreed to. Then Jim led his fraternity to raise funds by selling plastic stacking stools from Tigrett Industries to most students on campus. Soon nearly every dorm room had its own set of stacking stools, high shelves were suddenly reachable, and the SAE house was saved.[12]

During the summer between Jim's junior and senior year, he struggled to decide whether to enter the business world upon college graduation or attend law school. Either way, he wanted to be involved in significant business ventures. However, law school had an appeal and a clear sense of professional identity that attracted Jim. If he was going to apply for law school, he must do so within the next few months. Wanting to gain more insight into the practice of law, Jim secured a summer job as a driver and assistant for circuit court judge Andrew T. ("Tip") Taylor, a Union University alumnus. This experience enabled Jim to converse each day with a seasoned jurist, to be present for trials, and to gain a realistic insight into the everyday life of attorneys and judges.

It was also during this summer that Jim became interested in his own family history. He had often heard his father bemoan the fact that his father, William C. McAfee, had been swindled out of a fortune in the "oil well debacle" in Oklahoma. While waiting long hours for

Judge Taylor to finish meetings or court hearings, Jim would slip into a law library and attempt to research his grandfather's court proceedings in Dyer County, Tennessee, where William McAfee had sought unsuccessfully to regain his investment from the widow of his deceased oil investment partner. Jim was never able to resolve the legal process to his satisfaction, but it did cause him to meditate on the fact that the loss of one generation can have a tremendous impact on future generations. He realized, too, that the success of one generation can make life more stable and fulfilling for descendants. During this summer, Jim quietly resolved that he would be successful and build a stable foundation for his future children and grandchildren.

As Jim entered his senior year, he was more certain that he should not enter law school. There was something about the challenge of business and investments that was most true to his heart, his abilities, and his sense of life-purpose. Preparing for trials, writing wills and trusts, and doing legal research was not what would best motivate Jim to do his best. Somehow he would find a way to take his first step into the business world. Now his dream was more clearly focused.

Throughout high school and college, Jim had dated many girls. However, as he moved close to college graduation, he was not in a serious romantic relationship. This changed when he boarded a chartered bus for the annual Union University Concert Choir tour during the final semester of his senior year. Walking down the aisle of the bus, and clowning around as usual, he suddenly noticed an empty seat by Carolyn Townsend, the young freshman who had turned him down for a date during freshman orientation. As Jim smiled, she suddenly motioned for him to sit down by her. Jim did not know it—could not have dreamed it—but suddenly he had been struck by cupid's arrow! Later, Carolyn would claim that she "lured him to sit by her" and Jim would retort that she was "a desperate senior." But either way, things clicked, and over the course of the week-long choir tour, they became increasingly infatuated with each other.

Returning to the Union campus, Jim asked Carolyn out on their first date, only to discover that his car was out of commission and would not start. Desperate, he turned to his fraternity brother, Nathan Pillow, and asked if he could borrow his car for the evening. Nathan threw him the keys and chuckled.

What Jim did not realize was that Nathan's car was quite different from his. Nathan had recently purchased the car at a state government auction and it was a former highway patrol car. Built for speed, it was a Ford two-door coupe, pea-green, with a stick shift on the column. Nathan had recently added to the high performance engine a set of loud dual exhaust pipes that roared like a hot rod and could be heard from blocks away. Knowing that Carolyn Townsend was every bit a proper lady, Jim realized he was driving the wrong car for a first date. But love has a way of overlooking many things. In fact, Carolyn does not now remember the car or the embarrassment. However, Nathan Pillow is still laughing.[13]

What Carolyn does remember is that they attended a play at the university theater. Afterwards they drove to a local college student hangout called The Hut for dessert. Carolyn had pecan pie and Jim barely had enough money to pay the bill, but it was a magic evening that sparked a special romance. They both had found their college sweethearts.

As graduation grew closer, Jim was frantically looking for employment options. Jim's supervisor at JC Penney, Ed Poe, encouraged him to attend the J. C. Penney Co. Management Program and build his career with the nationwide department store. While considering this, Jim had a conversation with one of his older cousins—Jim's mother's nephew—Oscar Hilliard. Oscar was nearly a generation older than Jim, and Jim had always admired him. Oscar was living in Rossville, Georgia, a few miles south of Chattanooga.

He was involved in a newly emerging profession called *hospital administration.* Oscar advised Jim to seriously consider becoming a hospital administrator and assured him that he could make a stable and lucrative career with hospitals if he was properly trained and worked diligently.

As Jim explored this option, he discovered that Georgia State College in Atlanta had recently started a certification program in hospital administration. Slowly, Jim became convinced that his gifts and skills matched hospital administration and that he could make a contribution to the lives of many people by creating efficiently managed medical care facilities. Jim applied to the Georgia State University program and was accepted.

As graduation finally arrived, Jim looked back over four years of college with a great sense of happiness and good memories. He was departing Union University with a hard-earned degree, plenty of work experience, and a great number of friends, while most importantly of all, he had found love with Carolyn Townsend.

The day before graduation, Jim was sitting at the SAE fraternity house shooting the bull with his brothers, wise-cracking, and generally talking good-humored nonsense. Some of them were predicting who would graduate magna cum laude and which rare individuals would obtain summa cum laude. Others were discussing who would attend prestigious graduate schools and who would soon be getting married. Suddenly Jim jumped up in great glee and loudly chortled, "Boys, I really don't care! I'm just going to graduate and get the hell out of here!"[14]

The time had come. With such unrestrained vigor and determination, Jim was ready to enter a bright new world that beckoned him. He was determined to make his mark in life and be an outstanding success. The plan was not clear. But the future awaited.

Chapter 6

Graduate School and Engagement, 1961–1962

The hot summer of 1961 was a busy three months. Jim graduated with his senior class but had one more course to complete in summer school. Then, in August, he was to move to Atlanta to begin his one-year certificate program in hospital administration at Georgia State University.

Carolyn packed the belongings in her dorm room, said a fond farewell to four years at Union University, and returned to her small home town of Parsons, in Decatur County, Tennessee. Her father, Raymond Townsend, was a banker, and she had a summer job at Farmers Bank assisting Mr. Townsend in his work as a loan officer. These summer months would be a calm retreat before moving to Nashville to pursue a one-year master's degree in organ performance at George Peabody College for Teachers. Carolyn and Jim would be treading similar academic paths, traveling and dating between Atlanta and Nashville, and defining their relationship as they proceeded.

Returning to the lush beauty of rural West Tennessee was always refreshing for Carolyn. Since the early pioneer days, the ancestral roots of both her mother's family, the Malins, and her father's clan, the Townsends, had been planted in this rich alluvial soil skirting the winding Tennessee River.

Exactly a century before Carolyn's college graduation, her maternal great-grandfather, James Malin, had been wrenched away from his wife and children and thrust into the cauldron of the American Civil War. He joined a Tennessee Confederate regiment, and a few months later, in April 1862, was killed at the savage Battle of Shiloh. In this two-day slaughter on the border of Tennessee and

Mississippi, a total of 23,746 young men lost their lives. Much struggle followed for the Malin family after James's death as they faced the difficult years of Southern Reconstruction. Finally, during the 1920s, James's son, William David Malin, and his wife, Luty Wesson Malin, moved from their home in Holladay, Tennessee, to Parsons, Tennessee.[1]

Parsons was a young and expanding village formed in 1889 when the tracks of the new Tennessee Midland Railroad company were laid across Decatur County. A depot, water tank, storage yard, and livestock pens were hastily built, and a small town sprang to life. The railroad gave new promise of prosperity and commerce for this region. William Malin followed this hope and soon developed a successful farm and became a partner in a new cotton gin in Parsons.

Carolyn's father's family, the Townsends, originally settled further west in Dyer County, Tennessee, living in close proximity to the McAfee family as the twentieth century began. Whether the two families knew each other during these days is unknown. Soon, however, Carolyn's paternal grandparents, Eli Mansfield Townsend and Cordelia Harrison Townsend, moved from Dyer County to Decatur County. Settling in the small community of Hog Creek, twenty miles north of Parsons, Mansfield and Cordelia had eleven children to feed and support.

Carolyn's father, Raymond Clay Townsend, was the seventh child, sandwiched in the middle of the pack. Later in life he would say, "I was the runt of the family—sick and small—but I outlived them all." He would die at age ninety-eight.

When Raymond was a teenager, his father, Mansfield, moved the family from Hog Creek to Parsons, five miles west of the Tennessee River. As Mansfield and Cordelia traveled the twenty miles south to survey the land and find a new homestead, they rounded a corner, and Cordelia was instantly mesmerized by a two-story white house with broad porches, framed by shade trees and rich farmland. Though several of her children were now grown, she instantly knew that this was where she wanted to raise the rest of her brood and live out her years. Mansfield bought the property and began to farm the land. In time, he supplemented his farming income by buying a general store. A busy and industrious man, he also served as a purchasing agent for timber companies, selecting acres of trees to be cut and processed into lumber.

Mansfield raised his boys to work hard, and though Raymond was quiet and the runt, he was expected to carry his load. The Townsend boys often helped their father in the timber business, which was difficult and dangerous. Felling trees and transporting large logs had killed and maimed many men. Though this was not child's work, Raymond learned to clear land early in his life.

Amidst hard labor, however, Mansfield and Cordelia also made it possible for their children to go to school. Raymond exhibited a natural love for study and book learning. When he graduated from high school in Parsons, he was determined to attend West Tennessee State Normal School, now the University of Memphis. He dreamed of becoming a teacher; however, after two years of college, tuition payments became impossible, and he dropped out of college to earn a living.

Returning home, Raymond taught in several small country schools near Parsons. Then he moved briefly to Jackson, Tennessee, to work with an older brother, Wilburn Townsend, in the insurance business. Soon, however, Wilburn relocated his insurance agency to Parsons, and Raymond decided that, "all roads lead home." Raymond quickly discovered that insurance was difficult to sell in a small town in the early 1930s at the height of the Great Depression. He was fortunate to soon be appointed Parsons's postmaster and decided to settle down with a secure job in hand.

Still a bachelor, Raymond soon became reacquainted with a young woman he had known in high school, Sophia Marie Malin. The only child of William and Luty Malin, she was now a teacher in the Parsons school system. Both Raymond and Sophia attended the Baptist church, shared common intellectual interests, and were committed to the community and to teaching. Soon a friendship became a romance. When they were married, Raymond built a home on land that he had cleared years before as a teenager working in his father's timber business. They lived in this home for the rest of their lives.

In future years, Raymond became one of the best-known figures in Parsons. Everyone had business to transact at the post office, and Raymond, though quiet and reserved, enjoyed greeting people, learning names, and weaving together family connections. Later, in the early 1950s, Raymond joined in a partnership with his brother, Hobart, who was president of the Farmers Bank. He remained a banker until his retirement at age seventy-seven.

Reflecting on her father, Carolyn stated: "Daddy's theme in life was 'Be who you are!' and 'Do your best!' He was not flashy or political but he knew everybody and accepted them as they were. In recent years I have met people in Parsons who came up to me and said: 'Your daddy believed me and trusted me. He gave me a loan I desperately needed when I had nothing to back up the loan. He knew it and I knew it. But he gave me a chance. And that chance made all the difference in my life.'"

Raymond and Sophia Townsend taught their daughter by example to be kind, generous, and accepting of others. Quiet and humble, they modeled a spirit of graciousness that would enable Carolyn to later have significant leadership and influence in shaping important institutions, as well as supporting educational and theological causes. She was simply, but profoundly, taught to "be who you are" and to help others in need.

Jim first met Carolyn's parents when they drove to Jackson to visit their daughter shortly before college graduation. Carolyn had told her parents about her budding relationship with Jim. Raymond asked Jim to join them for dinner. It was a good evening of becoming acquainted. Following graduation when Carolyn moved home, Jim began visiting Parsons on the weekends. He soon struck up a particularly close friendship with Carolyn's grandmother, Mama Malin.

Raymond and Sophia could soon tell that their daughter was falling in love with Jim. Over the summer Jim and Carolyn began to discuss the possibility of becoming engaged. Not having money for an engagement ring or sure plans for his vocational future, Jim decided to give Carolyn his SAE fraternity pin before he left for Atlanta in September. *Pinning a girl* in the 1960s was a formal way of saying, "This is a serious relationship and a diamond is soon forthcoming." When Carolyn shared this exciting news with her parents, her mother smiled and quipped, "You've got a pin, young lady, but we don't want a wedding before a graduation diploma." Jim assured her parents that they would not hear wedding bells for at least another year.

As Jim moved to Atlanta, Carolyn settled into her organ studies with Dr. Scott Withrow. Her former organ teacher and mentor at Union University, Dr. John Hughes, had recommended Dr. Withrow. Dr. Hughes was a bachelor and was called "Papa John" by all of his students because of the way that he parented them. He was an excellent musician and caring mentor. However, when Carolyn encountered Dr. Withrow at Peabody, she knew that she had to step up to another level of excellence and performance. Dr. Withrow exposed her to a much broader breadth of music. He demanded and received her respect.

As Carolyn pondered her future in music, she increasingly realized that her natural calling was to follow her professor mentors and become a teacher. Yet, she also knew that if she were soon married, her ability to teach at a university would be dependent on where Jim was employed in hospital administration. For the moment, she decided to focus on this one wonderful year of musical training and leave the future open to circumstance and God's leadership.

Further south in the rapidly growing metropolis of Atlanta, Jim was trying to survive financially and still stay in frequent touch with Carolyn. Jim's aunt, Ruby McAfee Stallings, and her husband, Tommy Stallings, gave Jim $300 to make ends meet until he could find a job. Jim never forgot this caring gift. It made the initial weeks of his stay in Atlanta possible.

While his classroom work was at Georgia State University, Jim's real education was taking place in the chaos and trauma of his first hospital internship assignment at Grady Memorial Hospital. Deep in the depths and dregs of Atlanta, Grady Memorial Hospital was known as the best emergency and trauma care center in Georgia and was the prime hospital for dealing with indigent care. Every shape and size of humanity walked through the admitting rooms of what Jim called "ol' Grady horsepital."

During his first semester, Jim was initiated into hospital care when he was designated the admitting officer in the emergency room. A wide-eyed young buck from rural Tennessee suddenly saw "stabbins and shootins" every night. He frequently decided if a critically wounded person bleeding and screaming was qualified for admission into the trauma ward. Jim would tell hair-raising stories about these days for the rest of his life.[2]

Most difficult for Jim was dealing with those people who were drunk. He often chuckled about the lady who came in late one night looking for the "Peter Rabbit clinic." Finally, Jim realized between slurred phrases that she was looking for the pediatric clinic. Amidst the drunks, the punks, the motorcycle gangs, and the desperately destitute, the hospital security guards became Jim's best friends. This was a different kind of education from the one he had received at Union University. He was learning much about basic humanity, and he was understanding even more about compassion and ministry.

Jim was also discovering what it is to be sleep deprived. Working nights at Grady Hospital and then attending Georgia State classes in the daytime, he often functioned on three to four hours of sleep. Though he occasionally grabbed a nap in the interns' apartment at the hospital, he often kept himself awake through sheer determination, cigarettes, and black coffee. It was a difficult life.

On the occasional weekends that Jim did not work, he counted up his dollar bills, estimated if he had enough money to drive to Nashville, and headed north on narrow pre-interstate highways. Many nights he pulled off the road into a truck stop to take a catnap. Then he would resume driving for six hours through Chattanooga and on to Nashville. Frequently crossing the Cumberland Plateau at midnight or cresting the two-thousand-foot-high Monteagle, he would drive through thick fog or early snow flurries. On one occasion he drove with the windows down and his head sticking out the window, straining for better visibility. It was the kind of thing that only a young man deeply in love would do. But he liked the adventure, and he was more than glad to be out of Atlanta and headed home to Tennessee.

During the Thanksgiving holiday, Jim and Carolyn drove together to Jackson for a nostalgic walk on the Union University campus. Continuing downtown, they soon were looking through the display window of Rowe Jewelry Store. Suddenly the purchase of an engagement ring was being discussed. This was the moment that Carolyn knew that their relationship was real. In that same instant, Jim wished that he still had Aunt Ruby and Uncle Tommy's three hundred dollars.

As Thanksgiving ushered in the Christmas season, Jim drove back to Atlanta, and Carolyn returned to Nashville for the final days of the fall semester. A few weeks later, Carolyn returned home to Parsons, and on December 15, 1961, drove her father's Chevrolet Impala to Jackson to attend a morning concert at her alma mater.

Returning home that afternoon, she topped a steep hill and confronted a dump truck carrying a heavy load of coal careening into her lane. Before she could react, the truck struck the front of her car and she lost consciousness.

One of Carolyn's uncles happened to pass the site of the wreck. Recognizing her car, he stopped as the ambulance was arriving. Seeing her limp form, he barely recognized her. Covered as she was in black coal dust and bleeding from facial lacerations, he thought she was dead. However, Carolyn was fortunate. Though she did sustain a serious concussion and some minor facial cuts requiring sutures, no bones were broken and no permanent injury sustained. In a day before seat belts and air bag restraints, she miraculously survived.

Learning of the wreck, Jim set record time driving from Atlanta to the hospital in Jackson. Once assured that her life was not in danger and that she would soon recover, Christmas took on new cheer and delightful hope again. However, Carolyn would spend Christmas in the hospital.

Though Jim and Carolyn knew they were committed to engagement, Jim had not yet talked with Mr. Townsend to ask for his daughter's hand in marriage hoping that the Christmas spirit would set the tone and aid his mission. Jim visited with Carolyn's parents and they gave him their blessing. Standing by a hospital bed on Christmas day, Jim pulled a small box from his pocket and gave Carolyn the most precious Christmas gift she would ever receive—a diamond ring and a heart full of love.

Not many hospital administrators can claim to have proposed to their bride standing by a hospital bed. But the moment was a fitting symbol for their future. Jim and Carolyn would join their lives together unified in a desire to help others through medical care and quality hospital service. On Christmas day in 1961, all of these themes blended together in Jackson, Tennessee.

Chapter 7

The First Years of Marriage: "To Make a Difference," 1962–1969

Carolyn was released from the hospital on December 28, 1961. However, several months of convalescence were required before she returned to her graduate work at Peabody. Fortunately, none of her injuries had impaired her ability to play the organ.

Jim returned to Atlanta shortly after Christmas and prepared for his second semester of certification training. Transferring from the boot camp of Grady Memorial Hospital, he was assigned to work in the business department of Spalding County Hospital in Griffin, Georgia. He lived in a resident's apartment in the hospital and was soon discovering his true talents and strengths: personnel supervision, financial management, and business administration.

When Carolyn was able to return to Peabody, she was immediately faced with several major decisions. When she met with her advisor, she realized that because of her extended physical recovery, she could not graduate in May, but rather in August 1962. However, she was determined not to delay her wedding on September 1 of that year at First Baptist Church of Parsons. Her spirit and confidence were further buoyed when she received an unexpected invitation to interview for a faculty position in the Department of Music at Tift College in Forsyth, Georgia. Carolyn had always assumed that she would teach organ at a university. However, she now decided to delay her professional goals until after the wedding and until Jim could discern where he would next be located. Though delighted with Tift College's interest, she declined the invitation.

The spring and early summer of 1962 passed quickly, and Jim approached the final leg of his hospital administration certification training: a six-month residency program under the supervision of a veteran hospital administrator. Jim was fortunate to be assigned to the Albemarle Hospital in Elizabeth City, North Carolina, under the mentorship of Mr. Bob Jeffries. Jim would serve with Mr. Jeffries from July through December of 1962.

Bob Jeffries and Jim hit it off immediately. Bob's first impressions of Jim were positive, and years later he remarked, "Let me tell you something. When I met Jim it was like I had known him forever. There was no question that he would be a great guy to work with. We had an assistant hospital administrator position open due to a recent resignation and, prepared or not, Jim filled that slot."[1]

In July 1962, Jim moved from Atlanta to the coast of North Carolina to begin work at Albemarle Hospital. He rented an upstairs apartment in Elizabeth City and prepared it for Carolyn's arrival in September. Soon he was also immersed in helping Carolyn plan the details of the wedding.

One of Jim's first decisions was to select his best man. He had friends galore, and many of these young men had stood by him through thick and thin. However, when this special moment came, Jim asked his father to be his best man.

As recollected earlier, Jim and his dad, JT, had sometimes experienced moments of misunderstanding. Jim had struggled with the issue of being the younger son and often wondered if he had received his father's blessing and approval. For his part, JT had also wrestled with how to best express affirmation to a son who was quite different from him. One thing had always been clear, though: Jim's father loved Jim, and Jim loved his father. Sometimes love is difficult to express in the closest of relationships. However, the bond of mutual commitment and affection between father and son was never in doubt.

Carolyn soon asked her cousin and childhood friend, Patricia Townsend Chumney, to be her matron of honor. She also selected her cousin, Wanda Townsend, and her two college roommates, Mary Allcock and Schelley Childress, to be bridesmaids. The wedding plans were coming together.

As the day of the wedding approached, Jim was able to wrangle a full week away from work in North Carolina. As he drove from Elizabeth City to Parsons, he reviewed his list of groomsmen: Jim's brother, Bill; his fraternity brother, Bill Brown; his childhood friend, Matt Tomlin; and Carolyn's cousin, Edwin Townsend. These were great guys but Jim knew they could not be trusted when it came to playing creative wedding jokes. Jim decided that as soon as he arrived in Parsons, he must find someplace to hide his car! A locked garage was soon secured.

On the day of the wedding, Carolyn remembers that, "it rained like cats and dogs." However, by the time Carolyn's college mentor, Dr. Hughes, began the organ prelude at 4:30 p.m., the rain had stopped and Jim had arrived under guard at the church. As Jim watched a radiantly beautiful Carolyn walk down the aisle on her father's arm, he knew that he was receiving the greatest gift that life could offer him. Two families—the McAfees and the Townsends—were blending together, merging the journeys, the stories, and the traditions of countless centuries. Amidst the age-old traditions of a Christian wedding service, the soaring strains of classical music, the wedding homily, and the giving and receiving of vows and rings, time briefly stood reverently still and all was beauty. As Jim and Carolyn were pronounced "husband and wife together" and turned to recess down the aisle, they knew that they had experienced the most important moment of their life. They would always be united from this day forward. And they would face their future together.

Despite the lengths he had gone to, Jim's friends still managed to find his car and slathered it with paint and shaving cream. Yet Jim had outsmarted them—the day before the wedding, Mr. Townsend had offered for Jim and Carolyn to travel on their honeymoon in his new, air-conditioned, Chevrolet Impala. Now Jim had the last laugh as they ran from the church, jumped in the Townsends' car, and left Jim's car forlorn and decorated in the Townsends' locked garage.

Jim and Carolyn spent a short honeymoon in "Music City"—Nashville—then they rushed back to Parsons to pack Carolyn's possessions and wedding gifts. While driving to Parsons they spent the night at a Holiday Inn in Manchester, Tennessee. The next morning, as they drove out of town, Carolyn spotted the small Coffee County Hospital, framed and shaded by beautiful trees. Thinking about their evolving and uncertain future, she let her fantasies drift into words and said, "Jim, I hope that one day you can direct a hospital just like this one." Young marriages always find their symbols of hope and longing.

Arriving in Parsons they crammed Carolyn's possessions into every square inch of Jim's car and started the long trek toward the Atlantic Ocean. Two days later they arrived in Elizabeth City late on a Sunday afternoon. Jim began work early Monday morning and their new life together began in earnest.

Many years later, at age eighty, Bob Jeffries would reflect on his brief six months of supervising Jim at the Albemarle Hospital: "Jim had not been married long. He had a beautiful wife and they got along great. You could tell they were in love. Jim also had an unusually strong work ethic. You could be sure he would get the job done. He got along well with everyone. He always handled himself in a professional manner. He was astute and had an exceptional ability to read people. This amazed me. You could tell that Jim was going to make something of himself."[2]

Several months later Jim received a telephone call from a small hospital located between Nashville and Chattanooga. The chairman of a search committee seeking a new hospital administrator told Jim that he had been recommended to them by Georgia State University. The hospital was Coffee County Hospital, the same hospital that Carolyn had glimpsed through the car window four months earlier and had embraced with a heartfelt wish. Her wish had providentially come true. Several weeks later, Jim was interviewed and was offered the job. Immediately accepting this opportunity, the young McAfees made plans to start the year of 1963 in their home state of Tennessee.

When Jim assumed his position as senior administrator of Coffee County Hospital, he was only twenty-three-years-old. Many of the older employees, and especially the senior medical staff, did not know what to think about this young prodigy. Jim knew that he would earn—not demand—their respect. Jim would later laugh and say that just to assure skeptics that he was not the youngest hospital employee, he hired a teenager to be an orderly. Today, that orderly is now a physician and nearing retirement.

In 1963, Coffee County Hospital was a fifty-bed facility with a small, adjacent nursing home. Though Manchester is the county seat of Coffee County, nearby Tullahoma is the largest city in the county. This meant that the citizens of Tullahoma also used the hospital in Manchester as their primary care facility. This hospital was an important regional medical center.

As Jim assumed his new responsibilities, he faced serious problems. The county political system was often corrupt and dysfunctional. The hospital was dirty, outdated, and had poor fiscal oversight and operations. Jim rolled up his sleeves and went to work.

His first priority was cleaning up the hospital facilities and making maintenance a high priority. Hundreds of gallons of disinfectant were mopped on old floors and fresh paint brushed on dirty walls. Beds were replaced and surgical equipment updated. Soon a sense of pride returned to the hospital staff.

When Jim examined the hospital's financial records and audited the billing department, he was horrified. Thousands of dollars in unpaid bills and insurance claims had accumulated over time. Jim tightened the fiscal operations and aggressively collected delinquent accounts. Soon, the financial operations of the hospital showed a marked improvement, and the hospital auditors were pleased. Jim quickly became known, not for his age, but for his professional ability and his commitment to the job.

What endeared Jim most to the hospital staff, however, was his genuine concern and empathy for each employee. One laboratory worker, Calvin Harrell, reflected forty-five years later that, "Mr. McAfee always demonstrated integrity…He treated everyone with equality. He not only gained the respect of all employees and medical staff, but built within the entire staff that same respect for one another."[3]

People who knew Jim best recognized that his greatest talent was getting along well with a broad spectrum of people. Jim was genuinely interested in people of all walks of life. He was strict but compassionate. He kept a wary eye on the bottom line of the ledger book but was also generous with employees who were in need. He could be firm and decisive in working with personnel matters but was guided primarily by compassion and fairness. He always wanted to give the unemployed a job and would grant a second chance to an employee who had made an honest mistake. As a lab technician would later remark, "You could see a reflection of Jesus in this man. I am sure that had a lot to do with his success and his giving to others."[4]

As Jim focused on improving Coffee County Hospital, he also learned the importance of being an active civic leader. Jim agreed to lead polio prevention drives, chaired the United Way campaign, and joined the Rotary Club. He intended for the hospital staff to have influence within the community and he led by example.

Jim and Carolyn also joined the First Baptist Church of Manchester, where Carolyn frequently played the organ for worship services. In 1966, the church voted to organize and support a new mission, Trinity Baptist Church. Young couples were encouraged to become charter members of this small congregation. Jim and Carolyn agreed to transfer their membership and lend support to starting this church.

As Jim grew into his role as an able hospital administrator, Carolyn also searched to find her role in the community as a musician. Initially, Carolyn taught music in the elementary schools of the Manchester City School System. However, her skills as an organist could not be adequately used in this capacity. Soon, Carolyn focused more on serving as guest organist in many community churches and frequently played at First Baptist Church.

Having lived in apartments during the first months of their marriage, Jim and Carolyn symbolized a new settling down phase of their life by buying a house. From the time he was a paperboy Jim had had two dreams: owning a house and driving an Oldsmobile. Before long, the concrete for the foundation of the house was poured, and Jim purchased a dark green, two-door Oldsmobile Delta 88. It seemed that the "American Dream" had been realized.

As soon as he bought the Oldsmobile, however, Jim felt guilty that he had spent too much money on himself. He realized that there was not a musical instrument in the house for Carolyn to continue to hone her skills. One day, Jim saw an ad in the paper for the sale of a large electronic Hammond organ. A man in Shelbyville, Tennessee, owned a music store and had bought the organ to be played at Tennessee Walking Horse shows. However, he had soon discovered that the organ was too big to be transported easily, and he was now eager to sell it.

Jim secretly drove to Shelbyville to see the organ. Afraid to buy it without Carolyn's examining it first, Jim hesitated, but when the music store owner offered to have the organ delivered to their home on an approval basis, Jim jumped at this opportunity.

Carolyn was delighted with the organ but decided that the price was too high for their limited budget. She asked Jim to call the store owner and have him transport the organ back to Shelbyville. Obviously disappointed, the man drove to Manchester, and, as he did it began to snow. A beautiful, early winter snowfall quickly became a blizzard. Sitting in the McAfees' living room and gazing through a window at the pelting snow, the salesman finally blurted, "Ok, Mr. McAfee, I guess I am going to have to come down to your price. There is no way that I can move that organ in this snow!"

Jim chortled, knowing that he had struck a good bargain, and Carolyn was delighted with the gift of the organ. The Hammond is still in Carolyn's possession and is played and enjoyed today. A trait of Jim McAfee was emerging: driving a good bargain, at the right time, for a purchase of lasting value.[5]

After three years working as administrator of the Coffee County Hospital, Jim was approached by a committee from the neighboring city of Tullahoma with an unexpected offer. The citizens of Tullahoma had long wanted a hospital in their community. The post-war development of the Arnold Engineering Development Center had brought to the community many air force and NASA personnel. Tullahoma was growing much faster than Manchester, and the time had come for a second hospital in Coffee County. The committee asked Jim if he would leave his position at Coffee County Hospital to come and start a new hospital, guiding it through the design stage, then construction, and into full operation.

As Jim weighed this option, he realized that the political dynamics would be tricky. Jim was a new and popular administrator at Coffee County Hospital. And this hospital did not want competition from a second hospital in the county. Yet the need for another medical center was obvious and vital to the growth of the county. Above all, Jim was mesmerized by the vision of starting something new. After much deliberation, he accepted the offer.

At age 26, Jim became the administrator of his second hospital, the John W. Harton Memorial Hospital. Carolyn remembers his joy in "building a hospital from scratch," and as Jim would often say, "This hospital was my baby!" Yet amidst the joys of the challenge, there were the anticipated repercussions. The editor of the local newspaper grew angry and attacked Jim in editorials for leaving Coffee County Hospital. However, even he eventually came around. Within a year, this same editor saw that the move was positive for the community and became one of Jim's strongest supporters. Slowly Jim's critics came to see that two hospitals would strengthen the community and that both facilities were needed.[6]

The City of Tullahoma financed the construction of the John W. Harton Memorial Hospital through the sale of bonds. The hospital was designed to be three stories tall; the first two stories would be operational as soon as construction was completed while the third floor would be "shelled in" for future use. The construction was rapid and was completed in January 1968.

Along with the construction of the new hospital, another creative process was taking place. In July 1967, Carolyn began to feel queasy and light headed. Making an appointment with her physician, Dr. Ralph Brickell, she soon discovered that she was pregnant. Following the examination, Dr. Brickell left his office at the hospital and saw Jim waiting for him by the elevator. Jim immediately asked if Carolyn was pregnant. Though Dr. Brickell tried to hedge and save the surprise announcement for Carolyn, Jim immediately knew he would soon be a father.

Jim and Carolyn were overjoyed. Life could not be fuller. Giving birth to a baby and a hospital in one year was a bit much for a young couple, but they were ecstatic! Two months after the grand opening of the hospital, on March 21, 1968, Carolyn was delivered of a 10-pound, 2-ounce baby boy. Carolyn's physician, Dr. Brickell, immediately apologized to Carolyn for fussing at her about gaining too much weight!

Jim immediately called his father in Jackson, Tennessee, with a special surprise. A blizzard had closed traffic on Interstate 40, and the new grandparents were not able to travel to Tullahoma for the birth. Over the static of a phone line, Jim informed his father that he now had a new namesake, James Thomas McAfee, III. As Carolyn remembers, "Mr. McAfee had a complete conniption to see his namesake!"

As Jim and Carolyn McAfee would later assess their life, the years that they spent in Manchester and Tullahoma were "our ideal…some of the best years of our life."[7] These years built a firm and healthy foundation for the future. As they neared their thirtieth birthdays, they could look back and see that they had spent a decade learning the skills and abilities that would shape their personal and professional lives in the future. They had been blessed with a good education, a healthy marriage, a wonderful young son, a dynamic professional start, and a place to call home. Life was good and stable.

Yet, they now faced the future. What would their future dreams and ambitions look like? How would they live their life together? And what would be the passion and purpose of their existence?

Contemplating this moment in later years, Carolyn was asked, "How would you and Jim define your life-dream as you entered your thirties?" She thought for a moment and simply replied, "We wanted to make a difference."[8]

Chapter 8

Huntsville and Memphis, 1969–1975

On June 17, 1969, Jim celebrated his thirtieth birthday. Only a short time before he had been selected as the "Outstanding Young Man of the Year" by the City of Tullahoma. Jim's twenties were an incredible decade of accomplishment and fulfillment, and he knew his family could remain in Coffee County for the rest of their lives.

As is often the case, however, transitions from one decade to the next are a time for reflection and personal assessment. During this period of introspection, Jim was contacted by The Medical Center Hospital of Huntsville, Alabama, seeking his candidacy to become their hospital administrator. On paper, the hospital appeared to be a wonderful opportunity. It was a brand new-facility with state-of-the-art equipment in a community noted for engineering and space-age technology. Jim visited the hospital and talked with the search committee. His interest was sparked. Soon, Jim and Carolyn decided to accept the hospital's offer and moved across the Tennessee border to Huntsville. Now they would live no more than fifteen miles from where Jim's maternal great-great grandparents, Philemon and Emily Hilliard, had built their log cabin and tilled Cherokee land in the 1830s.

It soon became clear that this would be a new type of hospital for Jim to administer. The Medical Center Hospital of Huntsville was a private, investor-owned hospital. As a private hospital—not a city- or county-owned hospital—shareholders comprised the board. This meant that a primary objective was not only to provide medical care but also to make a profit for the investors. Many wonderful hospitals are investor-owned. But the board dynamic is dependent on the integrity, ability, and service emphasis of the board.

Jim had not been there long when he knew that he faced significant problems. Within a year, he realized his tenure would be short in Huntsville. Some of the board members and regional directors were urging Jim to engage in business practices with which he was not comfortable, and he began to search for another hospital to serve.

While this was a difficult time, Jim's experience in Huntsville did give him a deeper understanding of his profession and strengthened his commitment to honesty and integrity in the medical profession. During the course of 1971, he was approached by Medicenters of America to be its executive director. Its approach to medical care was unique and, at age 32, Jim accepted the offer.

Based in Memphis, Medicenters of America had been recently founded by Wallace E. Johnson and Kemmons Wilson, co-founders of the Holiday Inn hotel chain during the 1950s. Carolyn and Jim became particularly close to Mr. and Mrs. Johnson after they moved to Memphis, and both couples were members of Union Avenue Baptist Church. Seasoned and in his sixties, Wallace Johnson was a superb mentor. He had no children and loved to encourage young adults to live their dreams and make a difference with their lives. His own life exemplified this theme.

Growing up in poverty in Edinburg, Mississippi, Wallace Johnson had started picking cotton when he was seven years old and was a skilled carpenter by the time he was sixteen. But above all, he had the hidden and unique talents to become a business entrepreneur.

During the Depression era, Mr. Johnson managed a lumber yard and then worked for a building-supply house. When the Federal Housing Administration began financing single-family home construction in the 1930s, Mr. Johnson saw his opportunity to make an “honest buck” and do service for others. He soon became a major homebuilder in the Memphis area.

After World War II, when thousands of G.I.s returned to America and the Baby Boom ignited, Mr. Johnson formed a corporation to build hundreds of small houses quickly and efficiently, selling them for reasonable prices with low down payments. He became wealthy and later joined forces with Kemmons Wilson, Jr., the creator and builder of Holiday Inns.

Jim encountered Wallace Johnson at a pivotal time in his life and saw in him an example of a man who had made a fortune based on hard work and good ethics. He also saw a man who genuinely wanted to provide affordable housing and decent hospitality for the average American.

After making their fortunes through the Holiday Inn chain, Johnson and Wilson dreamed of helping senior adults who needed transitional medical facilities between full hospital care and residential nursing homes. They founded Medicenters of America to extend this form of healthcare.

For nearly two years, Jim labored to give the administrative help that was necessary for this new venture to succeed. However, Medicenters was an idea before its time, and the infrastructure of most healthcare insurance was not designed to adequately cover patient expenses for transitional healthcare. It soon became apparent that this venture would not be an option for the average American.

As Jim realized that Medicenters of America was not going to show significant growth, he was approached in 1973 about becoming the administrator of Neurological Treatment Center in Memphis, a hospital that was focused primarily on patients with brain, spinal, and nerve damage. He accepted the position. Soon, the name of the hospital was changed to Doctors Hospital, and it became part of Hospital Affiliates, Inc., based in Nashville—a large and rapidly growing hospital-management company that stretched across the nation.

It was not long before Jim's excellent work at Doctors Hospital was duly noticed by the upper management of Hospital Affiliates. Jim was invited to join the Hospital Affiliates national management team, with responsibility for multiple hospitals. At the age of thirty-five, Jim would no longer operate within the narrow confines of a local hospital and a specific community. He would report to an organization that managed many hospitals throughout the United States. This was perhaps the most significant turning point in Jim's professional career. He would now move from being a hospital administrator to a corporate executive.

As Jim made this professional transition, he was also coming to an age where his commitment to the church and his understanding of Christian faith was maturing as well. Becoming parents and raising a child often deepens family commitments to the life of the church. The church had always been central to the McAfees since their days of courtship. But now their faith and church experience grew even deeper.

Jim and Carolyn were increasingly committed to the life of Union Avenue Baptist Church. Carolyn frequently played the organ during worship, and both sang in the choir. Their five-year-old son, Tom, attended Sunday school classes that were taught by Lee Prince, their pastor, and his wife Robbie. Thus, the McAfees and the Princes developed close personal and family relationships, and Jim often talked with Lee about important matters.

Remembering these days, Robbie Prince characterized the McAfees: "Carolyn played the organ frequently. She was a wonderful musician. Jim was very proud of her and had great admiration for her talent...Jim always had an easy manner around people. He was easy to talk to and had a good sense of humor. He was always eager to tell you a new joke he had heard. And Jim loved his church and supported it financially well. He was always generous."[1]

Although Jim was a man of deep Christian faith, he was not overly pious, sanctimonious, or one who wore his faith on his sleeve. As one of his friends said, "He was far more a 'risqué saint' than 'holier than thou'!" People who had all the answers and talked in King James English frustrated Jim.

Like most Southern Baptist Churches, Union Avenue Baptist Church had a Wednesday night fellowship supper and prayer meeting every week. One night as the church family stood for the dinner prayer, a particularly pious gentleman was asked to say the blessing. With the most earnest and impassioned tones, he addressed God. Almost every sentence began with, "And Dear Heavenly Father, we just pray for…." After about three minutes of repeated "Dear Heavenly Father," one of Jim's friends peeked and looked at Jim who was standing in front of him. Jim had his hands tightly clasped behind his back and every time the man intoned, "Dear Heavenly Father," Jim would hold out a finger, carefully counting how often God had to endure "Dear Heavenly Father." It was driving Jim crazy and threw Jim's friend into muffled laughter. Jim did not like such ostentatious displays of piousness.[2]

Jim and Carolyn also preferred formal and traditional worship. They loved classical music and believed in a high and dignified sense of reverence. They wanted to honor God with their very best. Jim could be country and down home with the best of them. But his ex-Marine youth choir director, Lowrey Haynie, had instilled in Jim the meaning of respect and decorum. Jim was certainly not pious, but he didn't joke with God, either.

Theologically, Jim was a man of simple and uncomplicated faith. He had a true and personal friendship with God. However, Jim was also a man who liked to think, to ponder, to reflect, and to have the freedom to come to his own conclusions. He was taught to do this by his religion professors at Union University, and he had remained a Baptist because of the cardinal Baptist belief in the *priesthood of the believer*—the freedom to personally read the Bible, develop your own conclusions, and live within the Christian faith. Religious liberty was a very important issue for both Jim and Carolyn and would continue to grow more precious in future years.

Jim was undoubtedly a committed Christian, but his theological perspective might be best captured in an ancient Jewish prayer:

> From the cowardice that shrinks from new truths,
> From the laziness that is content with half-truths,
> And, from the arrogance that thinks it knows all truth,
> Oh, God of Truth, deliver us.

Soon after starting in his new role, Jim met his most significant mentor, Jack Anderson, then president of Hospital Affiliates. Jack was most responsible for training Jim to be a corporate executive and helped him learn the ropes of buying and selling hospitals. Jack would reflect on Jim thirty years later and say, "What made Jim McAfee good? He was trustworthy and competent, and those two things don't necessarily go together."[3] As Jack initially watched Jim's work at Doctors Hospital, he recognized Jim as having potential for increased responsibility in the national network of Hospital Affiliates.[4]

From 1973 until 1975, Jim's responsibility with Hospital Affiliates continued to expand, and his national travel increased as he assumed responsibility for more hospitals. He soon took his first trips to California, Washington, and Texas. Within a few months, Jim was in need of a larger staff and greater assistance. This was the moment when he met George Shaunnessey.

In many ways George Shaunnessey and Jim were very different from one another. Jim was raised in a deeply Southern culture, attended a Baptist university, and was a brother in a Dixieland fraternity, Sigma Alpha Epsilon. Jim loved pork barbeque, hush puppies, cheese grits, and a stout sip of "Black Jack" Daniels. George, in contrast, was the son of Irish immigrants, grew up on the south side of Chicago, and preferred hot dogs and Miller Lite beer. A Roman Catholic, he attended St. Louis University in Missouri and then completed a master's degree in business with an emphasis in hospital administration at Xavier University in Cincinnati, Ohio. Jim and George had grown up in different American subcultures.

Upon graduation, George was hired by Hospital Affiliates and given temporary management of a hospital in Chicago, before being transferred to the Memphis corporate office and assigned to work with Jim. For the next seventeen years, Jim would be George's supervisor, but they would work as a close team, traveling all over the United States together.

Reflecting today, George observes, "I grew up in the business under Jim's mentorship. Hospital Affiliates was not afraid to give a young person responsibility and then watch their performance." George will never forget that when he came to Memphis, Jim soon told him, "I am going to give you enough rope to hang yourself. Now do the job and make good decisions!"

When George did make inevitable mistakes, Jim would call it to his attention "but never in a scolding way." Jim played the role of advisor, friend, and teacher.

George credits Jim's bubbling sense of humor for much of the bonding that drew them together. Both young men loved to banter back and forth, and Jim could take as well as he could give. George recalled early in their relationship that they were driving in a rental car from Greenville, Mississippi, to Memphis. It was late at night, and Jim was tired and eager to get back home. George was driving cautiously across the Mississippi delta through small towns with eager sheriffs on the prowl for speeding cars. Jim kept saying, "Speed up, George, speed up! I want to get home before tomorrow." George obeyed and soon there was a flashing light in his rear view mirror and a Mississippi state trooper pulling him over.

Glaring at Jim, George reached for his driver's license. Jim started chuckling and said, "Shaunnessey, you get your Yankee butt out there and act like a gentleman." Jim paid the $45 fine.

The table was turned several days later in Richmond, Virginia. George and Jim always traveled light on short trips, usually packing one suit and several shirts they could carry on the plane. As they prepared for an important meeting, they ducked into a restaurant for lunch. Jim was always neat and dapper, and he had on his lucky suit. Soon the waiter brought them their salads and promptly dumped the entire pitcher of salad dressing in Jim's lap. As Jim squirmed and loudly protested, George began to chuckle. Just as Jim paid for the speeding ticket, George paid for the meal. As George would later wryly comment, "When you travel together for seventeen years, you get to know people on a personal level."

Of their initial years of working together, George recalled, "We grew up much alike. Jim's father and my father gave us basic security, but there was not a lot of extra money. We both cut grass and had newspaper routes to make money. You had to make your own money when you took a girl to the movies." This shared experience gave the two young men a common appreciation for hard work and the wise management of fiscal resources.

George also recognized that he and Jim meshed as a team because they agreed on basic group principles. As George explained, "In business what made us collectively successful was our ability to attract team-oriented people. Our approach wasn't about 'me' but about 'we'....We hired young folks who didn't have a lot of experience. We wanted young folks who were aggressive, wanted to prove themselves, and didn't have a lot of bad habits. We ended up with good people without a lot of turnover. What made Jim successful was getting good people who were over-achievers."

In addition to Jim's ability to build good business teams within hospitals or corporate systems, George also soon realized that a key insight into Jim was to understand his family commitments. In George's words, "Jim was a hell of a family man."

When they first began to work together, George was single. George recalls many times when Jim would say, "Can you cover this meeting for me. Got to get home for Tommy. It's trick-or-treat night...or little league night...or got to take Carolyn to a concert tonight." Family came first for Jim, and George did not forget the lesson as he entered his own married years.

Four years of living in Memphis flew by quickly. In 1975, Jim received a major promotion after working with Hospital Affiliates for two years. He was promoted to Vice-President for Operations of the Southeast Region. Hospital Affiliates had a total of thirty hospitals, and Jim would now be managing fifteen of those hospitals.[5] In six short years Jim had moved from being responsible for a small local hospital in Tullahoma to being a senior executive in one of the fastest-growing hospital corporations in America.

However, the promotion required that Jim move to Atlanta to be closer to a regional airport and in the heart of the Southeastern states. George Shaunnessey was also transferred with Jim, and they continued to work as a close team. Once again, Jim and Carolyn would be leaving their home state of Tennessee, while Tom would enroll in a new school in the Peach State. Young adulthood is often characterized by frequent transition, and the first fourteen years of the McAfee's marriage had involved five household moves across four states.

Chapter 9

Atlanta—Hospital Affiliates, 1975–1980

Jim was thirty-five when he and his family moved to Atlanta in March 1975. The Hospital Affiliates office was located in Dunwoody, and the McAfees purchased a home in nearby Sandy Springs. Amidst the chaos of unpacking boxes, establishing connections with the local community, and selecting a new school for Tom, they slowly settled into another chapter of life.

As Hospital Affiliates grew, Jack Anderson remained the chairman and CEO. Jim Buncher was the corporate controller and would later become president. As a regional director, Jim reported directly to Jim Buncher and Ray Stevenson, a senior vice-president.

Jim Buncher was originally from Illinois and was a certified public accountant. His true love, however, was business management, with a specific focus on financial analysis and planning. Reflecting on his early impressions of Jim, Buncher remembers, "Jim was a people person, and that was his strength. He could assess talents and skills for personnel. He could find the right person to fit a certain circumstance. Jim knew this and prided himself in it. He knew he had good people-sense."[1]

Jim Buncher also recalls Jim as a thirty-five-year-old whose demeanor was always professional and polite. Though Buncher was only a dozen years older, Jim always responded to his supervisor with a polite, "Yes sir!" and "No, sir!" Alongside Jim's jovial personality, there was also a defined sense of decorum and professional courtesy.

In terms of Jim's professional growth and challenges at this stage of his career, Buncher observed that, "Jim wasn't the greatest on the financial side of the world and he knew it. Jim knew that he wanted to improve his capabilities in understanding financial statements and analysis and he worked very hard at doing so. It was clear that Jim wanted to move up the ladder in hospital service and to have an impact on a broader scale."[2]

In relating to those that he supervised, Buncher noted that, "Jim was very even tempered. He could encourage and motivate people through his jovialness, particularly those who performed well. He was fun to be around. He could be a colleague even if he was your boss and he was able to clearly give his blessing to employees when they were doing well. But he could also get riled if someone really let him down or acted unprofessionally. You knew where you stood with Jim. If he disagreed with you, he would let you know."[3]

At the same time as the McAfees' move to Atlanta, Jim's mother, Frances, was rapidly declining in health in Jackson, Tennessee. For a long time she had suffered with chronic and ill-defined stomach and colon ailments, accompanied by periodic low-grade depression. Though Jim lived far from Jackson and respected his father's position as head of the household, Jim worried that his mother was not receiving adequate medical analysis and treatment. Suddenly her condition spiraled downward.

From March until July 1975, Jim drove from Atlanta to Jackson to visit Frances almost every weekend. Jim's love for his mother and their deep emotional bond was intense. As Carolyn remembered, "Mrs. McAfee had been his cheerleader all of his life." Now, just at the moment that Jim was breaking into the corporate world of national hospital systems, his mother was slipping away from him.

One of Tom's vivid early memories is traveling with his father to see his Grandmother McAfee during her final days. Tom was seven years old and had never witnessed serious illness or death. Arriving at the hospital in Jackson, Jim was informed that children were not allowed in critical-care rooms. He then asked for special permission for Tom to see his grandmother but was denied. Incensed, Jim decided to sneak Tom up nine flights of stairs in the rear of the hospital for a brief visit. With each step Jim became more incensed that hospital rules were sometimes not sensitive to the needs of families. Tom, however, was able to see his grandmother and treasured this final moment with her. This clandestine adventure of sneaking up hidden steps with his father formed a special memory.

Jim was with his mother when she died in July, and he was plunged into deep emotional turmoil. It was a multifaceted and complex grief. Jim and his brother, Bill, were frustrated by her medical care. Bill, as a physician, and Jim, as a hospital administrator, felt helpless to reverse her decline. Both boys experienced nagging guilt that they had not insisted that their parents pursue earlier and more aggressive medical treatment. People in grief are often plagued with guilt—legitimate or not—and the McAfees were no exception.

But more than grief and regrets, Jim was facing the first and most intimate loss of his life. This forced him to confront unavoidable questions and existential realities. As Carolyn would later remark, "Frances' death was life-changing for us all. It sort of brought us to our senses. It was a mid-life awakening to the reality that life is precious and short."[4]

Standing by his mother's grave, Jim made a silent pledge that he would not allow this quiet, helpful, and loving woman to slip into the anonymity of death. He would find constructive ways to honor and preserve her memory. He also promised that he would use his remaining years to create his own legacy, one built on his contributions to his wider community.

After the funeral, Jim and Carolyn discussed ways that they might honor Frances McAfee. They had just incurred an expensive household move, purchased a new house in the escalating Atlanta real estate market, and were raising a young son. Jim was advancing rapidly within his vocation but was not yet in the higher ranks of salary and benefits. They were a young, middle-class family with limited discretionary money.

Carolyn's thoughts turned to the fine organ in their church in Memphis at Union Avenue Baptist Church. It was a beautiful pipe organ but it did not have a set of chimes. Carolyn and Jim reflected on the symbolism of contributing chimes in honor of Mrs. McAfee.

As a boy, Jim had loved to hear chimes ring out from the belfry of West Jackson Baptist Church, summoning the neighborhood to worship on Sunday morning. But the sound of those childhood chimes came from a phonograph record played and amplified over a loudspeaker. While still in elementary school Jim volunteered to arrive at the church early on Sunday morning and play the recorded chimes. It was his special contribution and responsibility. Now, years later, Jim knew that it would be a fitting memorial gift to purchase a set of authentic chimes for their church in Memphis as a symbol of Mrs. McAfee's life of nurture and faith.

Consulting with the Minister of Music at Union Avenue Baptist Church, Leroy Summers, they discovered that the appropriate chimes would cost five thousand dollars, a lot of money in 1975 for a young couple. However, Jim, Carolyn, and Tom made the commitment to buy the chimes, and they were installed in the sanctuary organ. The beautiful peals of these chimes continue to enhance worship and glorify God to the present day. They are a symbol of a quiet and loving woman who brought her son to worship God and introduced him to Christianity by the example of her life.

This gift was also the first time that the McAfee family experienced the joy and satisfaction of philanthropic giving. They discovered that giving is often sacrificial, given not from surplus but out of costly conviction and desire. In the process, they first glimpsed one of the rare spiritual gifts that God was bestowing on them as a family—the ability to share and to make a significant contribution.

As Jim made his slow way through his grief process, he coped by throwing himself back into his work. He was now traveling more than ever to visit an expanding number of Hospital Affiliates–managed hospitals. One of his most interesting and humorous visits was to the furthest reach of his Southeastern region in the Commonwealth of Puerto Rico.

Jim Buncher asked Jim to travel with him to a prospective hospital in the Puerto Rico capital city of San Juan. Jim had not been to Puerto Rico and had limited knowledge of the hospital and its history. After landing, they ate dinner with a representative from the hospital. Sitting in candlelight in a nice restaurant, Jim was staring at their host's fine tropical suit when the man leaned over to pick up his napkin that had fallen to the floor. Suddenly Jim saw that the man was wearing a shoulder holster and packing a revolver "as big as a cannon." Jim's eyes grew wide, and Jim suddenly burst into sharing every joke and entertaining story that he knew—anything to keep the conversation light-hearted.

Later, as they said goodbye to their well-mannered host and walked back to their hotel, Jim exploded: "Buncher! Did you see what that guy had inside his coat! He was toting a gun! I mean he had a sure enough pistol. He could have blown us both away!!"

Buncher chuckled and tried to calm McAfee down. "Hold on, Jim! Just hold on! We're not in Atlanta. You just can't be too careful down here! Nobody's going to get hurt!"

Jim never forgot the occasion. And he never met with another hospital owner who was armed with a loaded revolver!

As the McAfees settled into the fast-paced life of Atlanta, Tom had many adjustments to make. In Memphis, Tom had attended first grade in a small, private, Lutheran school. Now in Atlanta, he was introduced to a much larger public school at Spalding Drive Elementary School. The school was excellent, and Tom soon settled in and made new friends.

However, as with their experience in former cities, it was the church that was central to the McAfees' community life. For the first few years, the McAfees were members of Dunwoody Baptist Church with Dr. James S. Chavis, Jr., as their pastor. The church was vibrant and developing a new Family Life Center where Tom soon became involved in children's baseball and basketball leagues. Carolyn was asked to direct a children's choir and often played the organ for worship services. The church was close to their house and was convenient for Carolyn and Tom when Jim was traveling during the week. Life soon took on a comfortable pattern.

Gradually, however, the worship services transitioned toward a more contemporary form of music and worship. While not opposed to contemporary forms of Christian music and worship, the McAfees were most comfortable within traditional or classical worship. They were soon drawn to the excellent music program at Second-Ponce de Leon Baptist Church in downtown Atlanta, under the direction of John Condra. Although the church was much further from their house, the McAfees' were willing to travel this distance for Tom to be involved in an exemplary church-music program. Favorably impressed with the pastor, Dr. Russell Dilday, they joined the church and began an ongoing relationship with this congregation that now spans forty years.

By 1975, Hospital Affiliates had become one of the major hospital management corporations in America. Jim coordinated the work and supervision of the expanding hospitals in terms of quality of operations, fiscal management, and levels of profitability. As Tom would reflect thirty-five years later, "This was Dad's time of building a corporate career and paying his dues. I am still amazed at how Dad handled so many hospitals with such diversity." It required much energy, focus, and long hours of work.[5]

While Jim stayed on the road, Carolyn kept the home fires burning and coordinated Tom's busy life between school, ballparks, choir practice, and homework. However, as Tom grew older, Jim was diligent in planning short family trips and vacations that provided extended time together and educational experiences.

In the summer of 1977, Jim was asked to investigate some possible business acquisitions in the western region of the country. Instead of flying, Jim bought a new gray Lincoln Town Car, loaded up the family, and headed toward the west coast. At the age of nine, Tom first glimpsed the rich midwestern expanse of corn and wheat fields, the grandeur of the Rocky Mountains, the solitude of the dusty central plains, and the romantic allure of cattle ranches, rodeos and cowboys. Tom's most educational moment came, however, when his father forgot to check the gas gauge as they crossed a desolate and sparsely inhabited expanse of Utah. The big Lincoln Town Car kept guzzling gas as mile after mile flew by with no sign of a gas station. Jim began to sweat and cross his fingers. Finally, down to gas fumes and prayers, a country store with one gas pump appeared and the big car coasted in. Tom learned much about geography and America. But he also firmly grasped the Boy Scout motto to "always be prepared."

With the months merging into years in Atlanta, Jim and Carolyn built close relationships with Jim's staff and employees. Each Christmas they hosted a festive dinner in their home for the staff, and Jim was personally interested in each family and what was transpiring in their lives. Jim was a shepherd who looked after his flock, but he was demanding as well. As Carolyn recalls, "Jim was tough on his employees but he was tough on himself, too. He was very disciplined and expected good performance from his team."[6]

As Jim and Carolyn approached their fortieth birthdays and entrance into mid-life, they began to appraise and analyze their life together. Carolyn remembers that the wake up call for her came one afternoon when she opened the mailbox and found a letter from their health insurance company. The letter informed her that because she would soon be turning forty years old, her medical insurance premium would be increasing. It was a symbol of the passage of time.

Jim was also becoming weary of constant travel and the responsibility of managing multiple hospitals in diverse states. The stress of crowded Atlanta traffic and endless hours commuting was draining. Often he would arrive home from a trip after midnight so that he could arise early the next day and have breakfast with Tom. Both Carolyn and Jim knew that as Tom entered middle-school years they would prefer to be in a smaller community where more time could be spent at home and with each other. They could feel the winds of change flutter and build intensity.

Jim, too, was at a stage of maturity where he wanted to earn more income for his hard work and loyalty. Jim made a handsome salary, but he increasingly wanted shared ownership in whatever company he worked for. He longed to be more than a senior executive. He also wanted to be a fully-fledged partner in a corporation. Though happy at Hospital Affiliates, he was open to transition and change.

This opportunity arrived with a significant call from Macon, Georgia.

Chapter 10

Macon—Charter Medical Corp., 1980–1987

In the early 1920s, a young man named William Arthur Fickling left his home in rural Taylor County, Georgia, eager to become a success. During the American Civil War his grandfather, William Hampton Fickling, had been a major in the Georgia 59th Infantry Regiment and a war hero in the small town of Butler, Georgia. Now, young William had this same desire for success and soon did exactly that. Having carpentry skills, he initially made his living through construction ventures. But in 1937, William Fickling partnered with B. Sanders Walker of Macon, Georgia, to form Fickling and Walker Realty Company. During the post-World War II economic boom, they created one of the largest and most successful real-estate firms in middle Georgia.[1]

When Mr. Fickling's oldest son, William Arthur Fickling, Jr., was born, he soon demonstrated this same propensity for success. An academic and athletic standout at Lanier High School in Macon, the young Fickling was a highly recruited college basketball player. Accepting a basketball and track scholarship to Auburn University in 1950, he excelled at almost everything he attempted. However, the most important moment of his life transpired when he was visiting at home in Macon during a summer vacation and managed to wrangle a date with a gorgeous young lady from Wesleyan College, Neva Langley.

Neva was a piano performance major from Florida, and soon after meeting Bill she became Miss Macon, Miss Georgia, and then Miss America in 1953. During Neva's senior year in 1955, she and Bill were married. After Bill had completed a two-year tour of duty

Kirby Godsey, Carolyn McAfee, and Jim McAfee
attend the 2003 Jesse Mercer Plaza Dedication, Atlanta, GA.

Jim McAfee introduces Jesse Mercer Plaza figurine, 2003,
Mercer University, Atlanta, GA.

Carolyn McAfee, Jim McAfee, Kirby Godsey, Tom McAfee, and Julie Crangle attend the dedication of the Frances Zoe Hilliard McAfee Plaza, November 2003, Mercer University, Atlanta, GA.

The Hilliard and McAfee families enjoy the dedication of the Frances Zoe Hilliard McAfee Plaza, November 2003, Mercer University, Atlanta, GA.

Tom McAfee, Tim Russert, Carolyn McAfee, and Jim McAfee
attend the 1999 Mercer University Executive Forum.

Jim McAfee and Bob Steed at the 2000
Mercer University Press Authors' Luncheon.

Jim McAfee, Jimmy Allen, and Kirby Godsey,
2000 Baptists Today, Judson-Rice Award.

Griffin Bell, Carolyn McAfee, David Hudson, Jim McAfee,
and Kirby Godsey attend the 2000 Advancing the Vision Completion
Celebration (Mercer University), St. Simons, GA.

McAfee School of Theology dinner, 2000, Atlanta, GA.

Jim McAfee, Carolyn McAfee, President Jimmy Carter, and Kirby Godsey attend the Inagural Convocation and Dedication of the McAfee School of Theology, Mercer University, Atlanta, GA, October 21, 1997.

Kirby Godsey, Carolyn McAfee, Jim McAfee, and Alan Culpepper attend the dedication of the McAfee School of Theology, First Baptist Church, Decatur, GA, 1997.

Jim McAfee, Kristian Anguelov, (McAfee School of Theology graduate 2001) and Carolyn McAfee attend the first graduation ceremony at the McAfee School of Theology at Mercer University, Atlanta, GA, May 7, 1999.

Jim McAfee and Carolyn McAfee at the Mercer Trustees Dinner,
December 2003, Macon, GA.

Jim McAfee and Carolyn McAfee
at the 2000 McAfee School of Theology Dinner, Atlanta, GA.

Carolyn McAfee and Jim McAfee, August 2004,
Mercer University, Atlanta, GA.

Alan Culpepper, Jim Sanders, Deen Day Sanders, Carolyn McAfee, Jim McAfee, and Kirby Godsey attend the 2004 Dedication of the organ in the Cecil Day Hall at Mercer University, Atlanta, GA.

Julie Crangle McAfee, Hyran Barefoot, and Tom McAfee
at Tom and Julie's wedding, March 6, 2004.

Raymond Crangle, Jean Crangle, Julie Crangle McAfee, Tom McAfee, Carolyn McAfee, and Jim McAfee at Tom and Julie's wedding, March 6, 2004.

Jim McAfee tends his marigolds at Big Canoe, GA 2004.

Julie McAfee, Carolyn McAfee and Tom McAfee
at the 2004 Mercer University Trustees Dinner, Macon, GA.

Bill Underwood, Stanley Roberts, Carolyn McAfee, Kirby Godsey
attend the dedication of the Townsend School
of Music at Mercer University, 2008.

Tom McAfee, Julie McAfee, Kay Samoly, Jim Samoly,
Carolyn Townsend McAfee, Alma Townsend, John Townsend,
Wanda Conger, Branson Townsend, Kay Townsend, and Charlie Conger
at the 2008 dedication of the Townsend School of
Music at Mercer University, Macon, GA.

Standing: Nancy McAfee, Branson Townsend, Kay Townsend, Tom McAfee, John Townsend, Alma Townsend, Charlie Conger, Wanda Conger, Jim Samoly, and Kay Samoly. Seated: Julie McAfee, Zoe McAfee, and Carolyn Townsend McAfee. The dedication of the Townsend School of Music at Mercer University, Macon, GA, 2008.

Carolyn McAfee, Julie McAfee, Tom McAfee, and Milburn Price celebrate the premiere of the Celebrating Grace Hymnal at Second-Ponce de Leon Baptist Church, Atlanta, GA, 2010.

Carolyn McAfee and Tom McAfee enjoy the Celebrating Grace Hymnal premiere, Second-Ponce de Leon Baptist Church, Atlanta, GA, 2010.

Zoe McAfee and Malin McAfee;
2013 Seabrook Island, SC; Enjoying Granna's house.

Bob Fisher, Julie McAfee, Carolyn McAfee, and Tom McAfee
at the dedication of the McAfee Concert Hall,
Belmont University, Nashville, TN, 2012.

McAfee Concert Hall, Belmont University, Nashville, TN, 2012.

Tom McAfee, Julie McAfee, Zoe McAfee, Carolyn McAfee, and Malin McAfee, Thanksgiving 2013.

Malin McAfee, Tom McAfee, and Zoe McAfee looking to the future, 2011, Seabrook Island, SC.

with the United States Air Force, he and Neva returned to Macon, and Bill went to work with his father's real-estate company.[2]

As the Fickling and Walker Company became increasingly successful, the real-estate firm branched into other forms of business. One of these ventures involved purchasing nursing homes and senior-adult care facilities. Bill became responsible for developing this new medical care venture and he formed Charter Medical Corporation. This corporation became a publicly held company and was soon listed on the American Stock Exchange.[3]

Within a short time, the nursing home focus shifted to acquiring and operating primarily psychiatric hospitals. There was a need for more extensive mental healthcare in America, and health insurance companies were offering good and broad coverage. Bill Fickling aggressively pursued this venture and was soon controlling a significant corner of this market. However, having transitioned from a real-estate corporation, he needed to build a team of experienced hospital acquisition and management professionals. Bill contacted Jim McAfee's immediate supervisor at Hospital Affiliates, Ray Stevenson, and offered Ray the position of president and chief operating officer, which Ray accepted.

Shortly after Ray moved to Macon, Bill Fickling asked him, "Who is the best hospital manager you know anywhere? I need him."[4] Ray replied that his former forty-year-old associate at Hospital Affiliates, Jim McAfee, was the best that could be found. Impressed by his youthful vitality and professional ability, Charter Medical Corporation was soon in touch with Jim and extended an attractive offer to become their executive vice-president.

Jim and Carolyn considered this option carefully. They had lived in Atlanta for five years and Jim had a bright future with Hospital Affiliates. Already he was managing the majority of their hospitals; however, both Jim and Carolyn were growing tired of the intensity of big-city life in Atlanta. Weary of long commutes and traffic jams, they longed for a more sedate locale. Tom would soon be entering middle school, and if they were to make a major move, this would be an advantageous time.

More importantly, Jim was able to negotiate with Charter Medical Corporation that he not only receive a significant salary increase, but also that he be a shareholder in the company. As such, Jim would not only be an employee but would have a significant ownership stake in this rapidly expanding company.

Jim and Carolyn decided to accept Charter's offer in January 1980. Corralling twelve-year-old Tom into the car, they traveled south on Interstate 75 to look for a new house in Macon. Tom remembers that the eighty-mile stretch between Atlanta and Macon seemed like "a vast nothingness" to a city-boy.[5] However, they found a house already under construction near the Idle Hour Country Club golf course. This would allow them to finish the house to their design and specification and also extend a faint hope that Jim would play more golf and engage in less work.

Carolyn was excited to be moving to a smaller town. Macon reminded her of Jackson, Tennessee, the scene of cherished childhood and college memories. Bill Fickling's wife, Neva, quickly took Carolyn under her wing and introduced her to new friends and the Macon community. Tom was enrolled at Stratford Academy, and the family joined Vineville Baptist Church, a church with a warm fellowship, traditional worship, and an exceptional music program. Life began to fall into place again. As Carolyn would recall years later, "Coming to Charter and to Macon was a great risk, but it was the best thing that ever happened to us."[6]

Jim quickly immersed himself in his new work. Charter Medical was a smaller operation than that which Jim had managed in Atlanta with Hospital Affiliates. In order to expand their hospital holdings, Jim needed to increase the corporate support staff. Perhaps Jim's greatest skill was being a team builder. George Shaunnessey, Jim's associate in both Memphis and Atlanta, soon joined the Charter Medical team as a vice-president and a regional hospital coordinator. These two men would continue to work well together throughout their shared tenure at Charter Medical.

As executive vice-president, Jim was in charge of all domestic operations, responsible for more than 70 percent of the total revenue stream for the corporation. Though Charter Medical was a public company on the American Stock Exchange, the corporation was struggling because of a lack of capital. Jim understood that they could not compete effectively if they remained positioned primarily in the broader medical-surgical hospital arena. Rather, they needed to narrow their focus and specialize in the area of psychiatric and addictive disease treatment.[7] Hospitals that focused on mental health were less expensive to run, the increasing need was apparent, and the health-insurance industry of that era provided generous coverage for patients. As a result, the number of private psychiatric institutions doubled in the United States between 1984 and 1988.[8]

Though aggressive in hospital acquisitions, Jim was a conservative fiscal manager. A member of the board of directors of Charter Medical, Kay Slayden, reflected, "Jim believed in good reserves. He was always shoring up reserves."[9] With a combination of tight fiscal management and aggressive and focused growth, Charter Medical expanded quickly. Within seven years, Charter Medical would grow from having fifteen hospitals in 1980 to owning and operating eighty-eight hospitals by 1987, becoming one of the dominant mental-health hospital groups in America. Charter's president and CEO, Bill Fickling, Jr., would also rise to be one of only eight Georgians on the 1987 *Forbes 400* list of wealthiest Americans.[10] Jim was a primary factor in Charter Medical's phenomenal success.[11]

As Charter Medical expanded, Jim, now a stockholder, would also become an increasingly prosperous man. Though his greatest financial gain would come in future years after he left his position at Charter, the basic foundation of his financial success was established during his seven-year tenure with Charter Medical.

However, as Jim expanded his professional world, he was also meeting an array of new friends who would significantly shape his future. One of these new acquaintances was Dr. Kirby Godsey, president of Mercer University in Macon, Georgia, a premier Baptist university.

Kirby Godsey and Jim McAfee first met when Bill Fickling hosted the annual Charter Medical Board of Directors meeting at a resort in Park City, Utah. Bill often invited prominent civic leaders from Macon to attend, and this year Kirby and Joan Godsey were his guests. For more than a century, Mercer University had been a major cultural and economic contributor to the community of Macon, and the Fickling family had a growing relationship with the university. During the days of relaxation in Utah, Jim and Kirby had several long conversations that opened the door to a deep and lifelong friendship.[12]

Raleigh Kirby Godsey was born in 1936 and was three years older than Jim. In some ways, Kirby and Jim were quite different in personality and ability, and they were an unlikely pair for immediate rapport. But in other ways they had much in common, which over time bonded them as brothers.

Both men were the youngest sons in their families, and each had been shaped by a nurturing relationship with his mother. Kirby's father had been killed in a car wreck shortly before Kirby was born. His mother was a strong woman who raised three boys in the depths of Great Depression poverty in Mobile, Alabama. Though Kirby's early life was poor, he was rich with a depth of love in his family and was encouraged to rise above adversity and fulfill his dreams.

A talented and spiritually sensitive young man, Kirby attended Howard College (now Samford University), a Baptist school in Birmingham, Alabama. With intentions of becoming a minister,

Kirby proved to be a brilliant and winsome student, majoring in religion and history. Upon graduation from Howard College, Kirby attended the New Orleans Baptist Theological Seminary where he obtained first a master of divinity degree and then a doctorate in theology. While at the seminary he met and fell in love with a new and vivacious organ professor, Joan Stockstill. Though she was a faculty member and Kirby was a graduate student, Kirby's ability to let no obstacle stand in the way of success stood him in good stead. Upon graduation, Kirby and Joan were married.

Not content with one doctorate, Kirby soon enrolled at the University of Alabama to earn a second master's degree in philosophy and went on to Tulane University to complete an additional doctorate in philosophy. He now knew that his future would be in teaching and academia, and he was more than well prepared.

Initially, Kirby was a professor of philosophy at Judson College in Alabama. He then became dean and vice-president of Averett College in Virginia. When he was forty years old and the father of four children, he became the dean of the College of Liberal Arts at Mercer University. Three years later, he was selected by Mercer's board of trustees to be the new president of the university. Dr. Godsey could not have crowded more academic success into forty-three short years.

When Kirby met Jim in Utah, a Tennessee hospital administrator who took great pride in not being an "egg-head academic" shook hands with an outstanding scholar and educator. Different as they were, both men were brilliant, insightful, and had their own recipe of talents and abilities to bring to a table of success. Both Kirby and Jim were highly motivated and had reached major professional goals by mid-life. They now looked toward the future with bright eyes and a keen sense of ambition. Above all, each was motivated to leave a significant legacy—one in business and the other in higher education. While Kirby was a liberal Democrat and Jim a conservative

Republican, they soon discovered that they agreed on far more issues than they disagreed on. They were an odd couple and a perfect pairing to collaborate on many future projects. But for the moment, they were two young men from Georgia meeting for a brief moment in Utah with great achievements behind them and exciting professional lives before them.

At the precise time that McAfee and Godsey were shaking hands in Utah, however, the Southern Baptist Convention was moving into its greatest chapter of discord and conflict since the days of the American Civil War. Both Jim and Kirby were cradle-roll Southern Baptists and had attended the denomination's institutions of higher education. The conflict would impact each of them deeply and would further solidify their friendship and direct them in shared pursuits.

Though a complex and multifaceted conflict, the emerging furor within the Southern Baptist Convention was fueled by four intertwining issues: interpretation of scripture, religious liberty, academic freedom, and power-politics. Each strand of this four-cord rope must be briefly seen and woven together.

Interpretation of Christian scripture has been debated since the Apostle Paul wrote the earliest existing book in the Christian Scriptures, the Epistle to the Thessalonians. Christians in every era have squabbled over almost every issue that scripture addresses. Hundreds of creeds have been devised attempting to bring various sects of Christianity into harmony and conformity. Yet dissension has continued to co-exist with harmony and common cause.

Baptists, who separated from the Church of England in the seventeenth century, were a rare breed of people; they steadfastly refused to write creeds that every Baptist must sign or adhere to. Fiercely individualistic, they insisted that every Christian should have the freedom to read scripture and come to his or her own conclusion about interpretation. And, most importantly, Baptists believed that unity could exist amidst diversity—that people who shared a common belief in the Lordship of Jesus Christ should be able to live in harmony with each other despite differences of opinion concerning scriptural interpretation.

A classic example of diversity in scriptural interpretation pertains to the creation story in Genesis. Some Baptists read Genesis and come to the conclusion that the world was literally created by God in six consecutive days nearly five thousand years ago. A singular man named Adam was created along with a singular woman named Eve. From these two individuals all human beings who have ever lived descend.

Other Baptists believe that the creation story in Genesis—while expressing divinely inspired spiritual truths—was never intended to be interpreted literally or scientifically. Therefore, current theories of the slow evolution of the human species over millions of years are not in conflict with the spiritual truths that are so beautifully told through the Biblical creation story. In other words, there is no essential conflict between science and theology.

Such examples of divergent strands of thought have existed side-by-side within the Baptist community for nearly four hundred years. This reflects the deep belief among Baptists in the religious freedom of individuals to interpret scripture to their own satisfaction as led by God's Spirit. The end result is that a diverse and opinionated group of Christians called Baptists are able to live in unity amidst diversity and cooperate in doing ministry together.

From time to time, however, a spirit of fundamentalism has pervaded the Southern Baptist body of Christian believers, and this fundamentalist perspective contends that all Baptists should believe alike concerning certain *fundamentals of doctrine* or unity cannot exist.

In the 1980s, such a spirit of fundamentalism and intolerance came roaring back into Southern Baptist life. The end result was that the fundamentalist party took political control of the Southern Baptist

Convention, including all six Southern Baptist seminaries and all Southern Baptist mission organizations. The Southern Baptist body—the largest Protestant denomination in the United States—was fragmented and moving in a new and uncharted direction.

In the opinion of Kirby Godsey and Jim McAfee, the new direction was a dangerous course to be taking. Jim might have been conservative in his business and political views, but he believed in the right of every Christian to develop their own theological perspective and still be a part of the Baptist family. Dr. Hyran Barefoot had taught Jim well in his Bible courses at Union University, and Jim would not surrender his theological freedom and religious liberty to anyone.

Returning to Macon from the rarefied air of Park City, Utah, both Jim and Kirby quickly lost themselves again in the rigorous and demanding obligations of their separate vocations. Their paths, however, would continue to cross and merge with greater regularity. Together, they would create a shared legacy focused on creating and protecting religious liberty, intellectual freedom, and academic excellence in Baptist higher education.

As he entered his forties, Jim faced another serious battle. He had lived the first half of life with great intensity, industry, and increasing stress. He loved his vocation and had consistently worked unusually long hours since childhood and his early-morning paper route. The man never slowed down and, as with most people, his strength proved to also be his weakness.

Jim loved to eat and craved good Southern cooking. Tennessee barbeque was the food of the gods and grilling a marbled sirloin steak was an art form. As a medical professional, he knew that smoking cigarettes inevitably led to disaster. Yet if he could limit his Winston cigarettes to a pack a day he was doing well. Jim was a man of the 1940s and 1950s; he loved old Roy Rogers movies, would follow John Wayne anywhere, and would not hear of changing his diet or forsaking his Winstons. For Jim, "a man's got to do what a man's got to do." But between the intensity with which he worked, the cigarettes, and his diet, Jim's health was feeling the strain.

Shortly after moving to Macon, however, Jim received an effective prescription to improve his health from some friends who told him about a small Atlantic Ocean barrier island named Seabrook, twenty-three miles south of enchanting Charleston, South Carolina. Only seven square miles in size, Seabrook Island had once been the home of ancient Stono Indians. The island was later named for Robert Seabrook, an English settler who landed in Charleston in 1679 and was convicted of trading with pirates on his island estate. Sold by his descendants for worthless Confederate currency in 1863, the island became a haven for people seeking solitude, rest, and relaxation.

A few weeks later, Jim, Carolyn, and Tom drove four hours east of Macon to Seabrook Island to spend a weekend. Approaching the island down a narrow blacktop road, they drove for miles under the ancient canopy of overarching live oaks draped with thick Spanish moss. Passing through the entrance gate, they were immediately embraced by a sense of serenity and solitude. Encircled by pristine white beaches and breeze-swept dunes, the deep blue ocean was framed by lush forest and green marshes alive with deer, fox, squirrels, egrets, pelicans, and alligators. If ever there remained a glimpse of Eden, this was surely it.

The McAfees fell in love with Seabrook and within a short period of time Jim placed a down payment on a small condominium that faced the beach at Pelican's Watch. With Jim's intuitive business sense, the condominium soon became a great investment, not only financially, but also from the perspective of health, relaxation, and healing. Seabrook became a retreat for rest and family time. It was a sacred place where the McAfees felt at home and closest to God. For a family that loved music and hymns, it evoked the lyrics of Isaac Watts: "*O God our help in ages past, our hope for years to come, our shelter from the stormy blast, and our eternal home.*"[13]

Macon also became, in a short space of time, a comfortable place to live. Tom remained at Stratford Academy through high school graduation and loved his group of friends. Knowing that their son was happy enabled Jim and Carolyn to put down deep roots and not see Macon as a temporary landing place. At mid-life, they had many good friends scattered all over the United States. Now they began to embark on new friendships in Macon that would traverse the years. Charter Medical also proved to be an unusual community because many co-workers also developed close personal relationships. For many reasons, the chemistry of Macon was right for the McAfee family.

Jim and Carolyn also were fond of their home. More than a nice house, it was a dwelling that welcomed you when you walked through the door. Though Jim's golf clubs were not often used at the nearby country club, he greatly enjoyed shaping and nurturing their lawn and garden. Like his father, Jim was particular about how grass should be cut, and he loved the look of a manicured landscape. Both Jim and Carolyn particularly liked flowers, and they enjoyed pruning plants and making their yard beautiful. When Jim could work in his yard, the stress of work temporarily melted away and he felt deep contentment.

Meanwhile, at Charter Medical, the creation of new mental health hospitals was escalating at a rapid pace. In six years they would build seventy-three new facilities within the United States and internationally for a total of eighty-eight hospitals. To use a football metaphor, Bill Fickling had proved a successful, able, and popular team owner and coach. But Jim was the quarterback who ran on the field, called the plays, encouraged the team, and "got in their faces" when things did not go as planned. As Bill Fickling would comment years later, "What I remember most is what a good manager Jim was. He was on top of things. He was loyal to me and I greatly appreciated his friendship. Jim was not a big shot. He was not enamored with his position. But he did have that fire in his belly to succeed."[14]

Jim was particularly a bottom-line administrator when it came to finances. Remembering his father now, Tom McAfee recalls: "Dad was very hands on as to what was going on at Charter. From the broad corporate divisions down to the individual hospital level, Dad knew the details of operations and made sure that goals were achieved. People shook in their boots when it was budget analysis time. Dad was both 'top-line and bottom-line' when it came to budget."[15]

Despite having immense responsibility on his shoulders, in many ways Jim found working at Charter Medical to be easier than his previous corporate positions. Charter Medical was the first organization that Jim managed where every hospital and facility was owned by the same company. No longer was Jim dealing with the myriad frustrations of trying to manage individual hospitals that were owned by multiple owners, boards, and organizations. Now, Jim could set up an organizational structure that was both uniform and effective throughout the Charter system. This model was much more to Jim's liking.

Charter also owned its own airplanes that operated out of a small regional airport close to corporate headquarters, so Jim's life was no longer consumed by catching commercial flights and rushing from airport to airport amidst Memphis or Atlanta traffic. Jim could tailor-make his travel schedule to fit his own needs and preferences.

Within the first few years at Charter Medical, Jim's personal financial situation grew incrementally. For the first time, Jim had emerged from being a middle-class citizen to a person with significant financial means. Bill Fickling had made a fortune in a short time through the rapid growth of Charter Medical, but he was generous and willing to share significant profit with his senior executives and shareholders. This positive change in Jim and

Carolyn's life did not show itself in sudden lifestyle change or ostentatious spending. Rather, they slowly expanded into pursuits that had long interested them and were good for their marriage and family.

Jim was, in the truest sense, an entrepreneur. Now he had the start-up capital to experiment with small business ventures of his own. During the six years that Jim lived in Macon, he started a barbecue restaurant, *Daniel's Tennessee Smoke Barbecue,* in Atlanta. He also purchased five radio stations in Macon and Gordon, Georgia, as well as in his hometown of Jackson, Tennessee. None of these ventures resulted in great financial gain, but equally none were failures, and they all offered safe ventures for Jim to play with. Jim did not mind rolling the dice as long as it was not a lose-the-farm risk. As Jim's Scottish ancestors might have said, "The man liked to have his fingers in a lot of pies."[16]

As a teenager just getting his driver's license, Tom McAfee was particularly intrigued by his father's new venture in radio stations. Tom loved music, had an interest in radio technology, and, as he matured, developed a rich and resonant baritone voice well suited for broadcasting. Through radio, Tom and his father found a common interest, and Tom first built a professional bridge to his father working in these stations and learning the trade.

Another interest that the family shared was international travel. Carolyn particularly enjoyed family trips and venturing to many countries. To be able to see the great pipe organs in the cathedrals of Europe and visit the haunts of favorite composers such as Handel and Bach was thrilling. Jim developed a particular affinity for Great Britain.[17] He was intrigued by genealogy and wanted to discover more about the McAfee clan prior to their migration to the United States. These trips were of particular educational value to Tom and broadened his perspective and interests during his teenage years.

The McAfees' enchantment with and commitment to Seabrook Island grew stronger as well. Several years after moving to Macon,

Jim and Carolyn decided to sell their condominium at Seabrook and build a house on this favorite island. They both knew that wherever they might live in the future as Jim's career expanded, they would always return to Seabrook for vacation and rest. It was time to put down roots and prepare a place for eventual retirement and future generations. Jim and Carolyn worked carefully with an architect to design the house. Tom and Carolyn even installed the yard irrigation system themselves during one of the hottest summers of the century. This house became a labor of love and fond memories.

Yet as life grew ever richer and his financial means expanded, Jim never ceased to worry and to prepare for his professional and personal future interests. Jim sensed that the rapid expansion of Charter Medical could not be sustained at its existing rate of growth. He also feared that with the corresponding emergence of newly conceived Health Maintenance Organizations [HMOs], the insurance provisions for mental health treatment and hospitalization would be increasingly restricted. These ominous shadows lurking on the horizon worried Jim, and he began to conceive of contingency and diversification plans for Charter Medical.

However, what he did not foresee happening occurred on a Thursday afternoon in February 1987. Earlier that day, Jim's long-time friend and protégé, George Shaunnessey, had shared with Jim the news that he had been recruited by a New York search firm to run Foster Medical, a $300 million company in Philadelphia. George tendered his resignation to Jim and left immediately to fly to Philadelphia for his final interview. Jim and George had worked closely and effectively together for seventeen years and Jim was greatly saddened by this news.[18]

Leaving the office early, Jim drove home depressed and not feeling well. Tom had recently graduated from Stratford Academy and was now a freshman at Mercer University. Jim and Tom had agreed to drive together to Seabrook that evening to spend the weekend launching for the first time a new ski boat they had recently purchased. When Jim walked into the kitchen he found the house quiet and he realized that he was alone. Carolyn had gone to the grocery store and Tom had not yet returned home from practice with the Mercer Singers.

Slumping down to rest, Jim grew clammy, nauseous, and short of breath. Though he did not feel chest pain, he had an instinctive feeling of impending doom. He knew that he was having a heart attack.

Within a few minutes Carolyn returned home and found Jim conscious but desperate to go to the emergency room. She rushed him to nearby Northside Hospital, a newly built Charter Medical facility that had been constructed under Jim's guidance. Entering the emergency room, Jim realized that the doctor on call had given him a physical for an insurance policy only a few weeks earlier and had found him in good health. However, a few quick tests confirmed that Jim was having a major heart attack. Fortunately, an experimental drug known as a "clot buster" was available and was immediately used. The injection saved Jim's life. Unfortunately, a significant amount of heart muscle damage was incurred that would permanently weaken Jim's pulmonary function.

As soon as Jim could be stabilized, he was transported to Emory University Hospital in Atlanta for further evaluation and treatment. It was decided that he was a candidate for angioplasty, and Jim's partially blocked arteries were soon opened so that his heart muscles could receive improved blood flow. The angioplasty procedure was successful, and Jim's cardiologist ordered a long medical leave from work and stress.

Bill Fickling was particularly worried about Jim and insisted he take adequate time to recuperate. Bill visited Jim almost every day while he convalesced in Macon. However, Jim and Carolyn soon decided to retreat to Seabrook and their new beach house to rest, regroup, and come to terms with this new critical health reality.[19]

There is no doubt that Jim's heart attack was one of the most pivotal events in Jim's and Carolyn's lives and had a dominant influence on how they would live their future years. Reflecting on that moment, Carolyn remembers, "Before Jim's heart attack we had the world by the tail and everything was going great and then Boom!!!! Suddenly Jim is left with significant heart muscle damage…. It totally changed my outlook on life, too. A wake-up call. You're going along busy with life as usual and suddenly everything comes to a screeching halt. Suddenly everything was focused on trying to get Jim back into life."[20]

As Jim and Carolyn nestled into the calm beauty and seclusion of Seabrook, Jim slowly peeled back the layers of his life and looked reality in the face. Tom recalls that, "Seabrook was not an easy time at all. Dad felt like he would never be able to do anything again. He was physically weak and could not do anything but worry about it."[21]

Carolyn was always the center and the stabilizer of Jim's inner world. He could handle business with the toughest executives, but in the depths of Jim's soul, Carolyn was the emotional ballast that steadied his ship in the midst of a storm. Carolyn recalls those days at Seabrook as a time when "We didn't know what the future would bring. It was a bonding time. A deep realization that time is precious."[22]

Slowly, Jim became more confident that he would survive the ravages of this specific heart attack. But he also knew that the heart attack revealed that he had serious cardiovascular disease that would never go away. Whether it was a matter of heredity or lifestyle or chemistry could not be fully known, but it was clear that Jim had serious atherosclerosis and that to reduce this risk would require major lifestyle change.

Jim also knew that his heart muscle damage was extensive and irreversible. He would one day share with his son, Tom, that after his heart attack he was told by at least one physician that the likelihood of his living beyond another dozen years was not good.[23] This one factor suddenly brought an increased focus and urgency to his life. As Tom reflected, "Dad had three choices. First, he could simply give up and die. Second, he could choose the life of medical retirement and slowly wither away. Or, three, he could get back into the stream and make the next years the best years." For Jim, this was no choice. He might be knocked down temporarily, but he would find a way to stand back up and win the battle of life.[24]

When Jim was growing up, there was a plaque that hung in the homes of many American and British Christians that quoted the words of a dynamic English missionary, Charles T. Studd: "*Only one life will soon be past, only what's done for Christ will last.... for me to live is Christ.*" There is strong evidence that Jim and Carolyn reflected on the deeper substance of this quote and it gave them strength and resolve to embrace life and pursue their commitment to making a lasting contribution.[25]

The first thing to be discarded from the old lifestyle were the cigarettes. When Jim was in his first days of recovery at Emory University Hospital, he was taken into a surgery ward for heart catheterization. During the procedure, the doctors urged a semiconscious Jim to inhale cigarette smoke so that he could see on the monitor screen the sudden physical effect that one cigarette had on his heart. Jim stubbornly shook his head and mumbled, "No need. I am a convert!!"

Jim was, indeed, a convert! He never smoked a cigarette again. In fact, he gave away all of his clothes that smelled like cigarette smoke and bought a new wardrobe. He tried to avoid tobacco smoke in crowds and in restaurants. He became a true believer.

Jim also embraced exercise. Never athletic, Jim did enjoy walking, particularly on the long expanses of beach at Seabrook. Slowly Jim increased the length of short walks, gradually building his strength and endurance. In the future, Jim would not travel without packing running shoes and workout clothes. He bought a treadmill for each of his houses. And he took long walks outside regardless of the weather.[26]

Jim and Carolyn also talked about their future goals and aspirations as a couple. Shortly before Jim's heart attack, they had briefly discussed forming a foundation for the purpose of tax planning and also to contribute to special causes that were important to them. Now, after Jim's health crisis and near death, they returned to this topic. As Carolyn later reflected, "Jim had now come to believe that he was given a second chance at life and he wanted to take full advantage of that."[27]

Tom, too, realized after his father's health crisis that Jim was highly motivated to "give back to life." Jim had always had charitable and generous inclinations. But the existential encounter with near-death had now fully engaged the gears of philanthropy and contribution. Over the next few months the legal process was initiated to create the James T. McAfee, Jr., and Carolyn T. McAfee Foundation, and, in 1987 the foundation became a reality.[28]

After three months of rest at Seabrook, Jim and Carolyn returned to Macon so that Jim could receive more advanced physical therapy and rehabilitation. Jim's future employment at Charter Medical was secure, and Bill Fickling was clear that he wanted Jim to continue as a senior officer and board director at Charter. However, Jim was increasingly feeling uneasy about remaining at Charter Medical for several reasons.

First, with the advent of his health crisis, Jim felt that the senior staff might see him as more tentative and fragile. Jim was used to going full speed ahead and playing hardball. Now he sensed that he might formally—or informally—be shifted from being the true quarterback of the Charter Medical team to being an offensive coordinator, calling plays but standing on the sideline. Needless to say, this idea hardly appealed to Jim, and he tried to avoid entertaining it even as a possibility.

Most important, however, Jim's brush with death left him with a heightened sense of urgency. With whatever years lay before him, he now knew that he wanted to maximize his earning power and by doing so, heighten his ability to make personal and financial contributions to causes that were important to him. During his years at Charter, Jim had accrued significant personal financial wealth. Now he wanted to leverage and enlarge this investing power by launching into a new business venture where he would become the senior stockholder and the captain of the ship. But how this new chapter of opportunity might be approached and defined was still a mystery. Jim just knew that the tide was changing, the wind was blowing in a new direction, and he must change course to venture toward new challenges and opportunities.

Chapter 11

National Healthcare and Hallmark Healthcare Corporation, 1987–1994

A few months after his heart attack, Jim and Tom were cruising on their twenty-foot ski boat on the Ashley River between Seabrook Island and Charleston. Lulled by the lush beauty of low country South Carolina, Jim suddenly remembered he had not called Carolyn to assure her he was feeling well. Throttling back the engine, Tom glided the boat into Buzzard's Roost Marina to find a payphone. Carolyn soon answered, and she had news: a hospital company in Dothan, Alabama, had called repeatedly that day, eager to track Jim down. Standing on a dock in the marshlands of South Carolina, Jim did not realize he was entering the next chapter of his professional life.[1]

The call was from some nervous investors who were frantic to find a competent and experienced hospital corporation manager who would assume leadership—and significant ownership—of National Healthcare.[2] Based in Dothan, National Healthcare had originally been started by executives who worked for Jim at Hospital Affiliates in Nashville. Formerly a vital company with more than sixty general-surgical hospitals, the corporation now teetered on the edge of bankruptcy. Ominously, some of the corporate leadership was under investigation for engaging in improprieties. National Healthcare would obviously not be an easy situation to turn around.

The positive factor, however, was that if Jim did assume leadership of the company, he could buy stock at extremely low prices and become a primary shareholder. It was a high risk but also an unusual opportunity to make a significant profit.

As Jim pondered this option, he also realized that he was a man who had barely survived a heart attack a few short months ago. To now take such a physical risk seemed absurd. And yet he sensed that this venture could be the business opportunity of a lifetime.

Jim soon traveled from Seabrook to Dothan to further investigate the opportunity with National Healthcare. Gradually he grew more confident that if he were given absolute control of operations, portions of this company could be salvaged and restructured. Jim ultimately decided that he would invest his money and his life to either sink or swim with National Healthcare.

It was difficult for Jim to resign from Charter Medical in Macon. Bill Fickling and Jim McAfee genuinely loved and respected each other, and their seven years of working together had been rich and positive. However, Jim knew that to continue with his life's dream, parting was necessary. Tom was now a sophomore at Mercer University in Macon, so Carolyn and Tom would remain in Georgia while Jim rented an apartment in Dothan and lost himself in his work. Jim would later remark that this new challenge saved his life and helped him regain health and equilibrium.

The biggest battle that Jim faced was working with the multiple private investors who held stock in National Healthcare. Many investors believed that the corporation could not be turned around and made successful. In recent months, the company had been delisted or taken off the stock market because it was nearly insolvent and stock had dipped to seven cents a share. Many investors wanted to declare bankruptcy immediately.[3]

Jim did not believe in bankruptcy and began to radically change the company to demonstrate that it could return to financial health. First, he surveyed each of the company's hospitals scattered across the country to decide which properties should be sold or retained. In short order, the hospitals were pared from sixty to thirty-five, budgets slashed, and non-essential acquisitions such as the fleet of airplanes sold. As Tom recalled, "Dad insisted that they get back to basics and deliver true healthcare."[4]

Jim then relocated the corporate headquarters to Atlanta to remove it from a deteriorating relationship with the community of Dothan and start a new and fresh chapter in the life of the company. Finally, he recruited experienced senior administrators, as well as fresh members of the board of directors. This new infusion of leadership and expertise gradually brought National back to health.

One of the new members of Jim's senior leadership team was his old friend and colleague, George Shaunnessey. A year before, George had left Charter Medical in Macon to direct Foster Medical in Philadelphia. Soon after, Foster Medical was sold by Avon Corporation, and Jim saw an opportunity to partner with George again. Jim called George and talked him into becoming president of National Healthcare while Jim retained the title of chairman. This seasoned duo understood each other and worked in step like two old plow horses.[5]

Jim also strengthened his board of directors by bringing on two men with deep Alabama roots whom he had previously observed when they served on the Charter Medical Board in Macon. Jim Martin and Kay Slayden brought instant credibility and wisdom garnered over many years to the board of directors of National Healthcare and helped Jim immensely.

In the early 1950s, Jim Martin, Kay Slayden, and Bill Fickling were teammates on the Auburn University basketball team. Together they formed one of Auburn's most memorable teams, and following graduation later proved to be even more successful as business leaders. Dr. Jim Martin served for five years as the president of the University of Arkansas before returning to Auburn University to serve eight years as president of his alma mater. During these same years, Kay Slayden excelled in business and became president of the international Fuqua Industries conglomerate. Martin and Slayden now brought their immense talents to help Jim reshape National Healthcare and calm the jitters of nervous shareholders.

Finally, after moving corporate headquarters to Atlanta, Jim asked the board of directors to change the name of the corporation from National Healthcare to Hallmark Healthcare Corporation. Jim wanted to put the scarred history of the corporation behind him and selected a new name that would reflect an emerging quality and public trust.

Once Jim had relocated Hallmark Healthcare Corporation to Atlanta, the McAfee house in Macon was sold. In 1989, Carolyn and Tom moved to join Jim in Atlanta, with Tom transferring to the Mercer campus there. Jim and Carolyn once again moved their church membership to Second Ponce de Leon Baptist Church and it seemed that life had suddenly come full circle.

As Jim returned to greater physical and emotional health, so did Hallmark Healthcare Corporation rebound to new life. Within seven years, the stock price of old National Healthcare would soar from seven cents to fifty-four dollars a share under the banner of Hallmark Healthcare Corporation.[6] Jim's business dreams were coming true. More importantly, however, Jim was also being widely recognized as a major contributor and shaper of the hospital industry in America during the concluding years of the twentieth century.

Just as Jim and Carolyn were reconnected to life in Atlanta in 1989, so, too, were they reunited in their relationship with Union University in Jackson, Tennessee. In February 1987—the same month Jim had had his heart attack—his former college religion professor, Dr. Hyran Barefoot, was elected president of Union. Dr. Barefoot soon began to reach out to former students and alumni he had loved and respected over the years, and one of those students was Jim McAfee. As Dr. Barefoot would later reflect, "Jim McAfee was an interesting person, not your ordinary citizen. He was an average student. But it's not the 'A student' that often does well in life. If I had to choose twenty-five of the top people I have met in my life, Jim would be high on that list. He had a wide range of interests and a desire to contribute. I would tell him about things Union wanted to do and Jim would jump right in."[7]

Dr. Barefoot soon informed Jim of a financial need that Union University was struggling to resolve. One of the landmarks on the Union campus is the G.M. Savage Chapel. Construction on a beautiful forty-four rank Visser-Rowland pipe organ was completed in the chapel during the mid-1980s; however, contributions to pay for the organ had lagged far behind, and the lingering debt was a significant concern for the university. When Jim became aware of this, he and Tom made arrangements to meet with Dr. Barefoot during a Baptist convention in Atlanta. They surprised Dr. Barefoot with the unexpected news that they would like to complete the payment for the pipe organ as a gift in Carolyn's honor. Barefoot was visibly and emotionally moved by such generosity.[8]

Carolyn, however, was not aware of this surprise gift and when informed she was overwhelmed! It was a moment that brought great joy and celebration. Today, the Carolyn Townsend McAfee Organ at Union University is not only used to inspire worship, but also to train and produce future generations of young organists.

Soon after the gift was made to finance the organ, Carolyn discussed with Jim the possibility of also funding an annual organ concert series that would enable premier organists to be brought to campus to demonstrate skills and repertoire for organ students. Jim was enthusiastic, the funds were provided, and the first artist to play the dedicatory concert was Dr. Scott Bennett.[9]

Within a few short months, a third contribution was also made to Union University to honor Jim's mother. A new dormitory was under construction that was designed to have an attractive indoor area called "The Commons," where students could meet for conversation and fellowship. Because Jim's mother exuded a quiet hospitality, Jim and

Carolyn gave the funding for this space and it was named the Frances Zoe Hilliard McAfee Commons in 1990.

As Jim celebrated his fiftieth birthday, he had moved into a new era of not only making money, but of also contributing money in significant amounts. The combined recent gifts to Union University totaled more than one million dollars, which at that time was the largest gift made by a living donor.[10] This example set the bar for future contributors to the university. Jim and Carolyn were leading by example, and their example would inspire other Union alumni to follow the invitation of President Barefoot to "jump right in."

As Jim and Carolyn returned to Atlanta, they began to search for a place of quiet retreat away from city bustle, yet closer than Seabrook Island. Only an hour north of Atlanta, the southern Appalachian Mountains rise in beauty and prominence. Driving around these beautiful peaks and valleys, the McAfees soon discovered a resort community named Big Canoe.

Begun as a planned residential community in 1972, Big Canoe encompasses eight thousand acres that include three picturesque lakes. Nearly one-third of the property is set aside as wildlife areas and nature parks. Most of the residents commute to Atlanta or are retired. Jim's childhood years in Chattanooga had created in him a deep love for mountain beauty, and he instantly felt at home at Big Canoe.

After searching for several months for just the right place, Jim and Carolyn were drawn to a secluded log cabin situated high on a ridge. They purchased the cabin and began to spend long weekends away from work. Jim had found his place of rest and healing.[11]

At the same time that Jim and Carolyn's world was falling back into place, Tom was going through a time of young adult transition and searching. In his early twenties, Tom was concluding his junior year at Mercer and was a communications major. However, he was uncertain about his vocational future and increasingly less motivated by college classes. Tom was much like his father. Academics for the sake of academics was not a source of motivation for him. Though highly intelligent, talented, and curious, Tom was not excited by making stellar grades or the immediate prospects of graduate school. As a twenty-one-year-old, he wanted to find something tangible that he truly enjoyed and which he could develop into something successful and worthwhile. The McAfee bent toward practical entrepreneurship was stirring in his soul.

As a teenager, Tom had discovered radio and electronics through his father's brief foray into owning radio stations in Georgia and Tennessee. It was within the practical challenge of the radio and communications business that Tom currently felt most alive and motivated. More than just a business venture, however, Tom was particularly drawn to understanding and expanding the technical side of the McAfee radio stations. In an era when communications technology was rapidly changing, Tom wanted to be on the cutting edge of technology.

Tom's quest for state-of-the-art technology sometimes brought a business-minded father and a technology-motivated son into conflict with one another. Yet fathers at mid-life and sons in early adulthood are prone to disagreement and head-butting. Tom and Jim were no different and would have to find a way to give each other the freedom to succeed or fail. As Tom would later reflect, "As a young man, I wanted to be like my father in the worst way. We shared a lot of the same interests. Yet we had significant differences as well."[12] It usually takes years for a father to relinquish the idolatry of trying to make his son into his image and for a son to accept his father simply for who he is. This is an unavoidable dynamic of coming of age, but out of it can be borne the strongest of relationships.

Increasingly, Tom talked of leaving Mercer until he could better clarify his future aspirations. Finally in 1990, Tom and Jim sat down and had a father-to-son talk. With his reconnection with Union

University, Jim had recently bought a radio station in Jackson, Tennessee, that serviced the Union University community. Looking Tom in the eye, Jim said, "Why don't you take the next semester off, and go to Jackson and run the station until I can find a manager." Tom jumped at the opportunity and began a new chapter that would encompass the next seven years of his young life. Now, Jim and Carolyn would live in Georgia while Tom returned to the "homeland" of the McAfee and Townsend clans. Tom was maturing and leaving home to return to home. He would discover many things.[13]

One such discovery was a pretty and vivacious Union University co-ed named Julie Crangle. Julie was a communications major at Union and needed both a job and an internship. One of her professors, Dr. Mike Davis, telephoned Tom McAfee, now the new general manager at Q102-WZDQ, and inquired if one of his students could work as an intern at the station. Tom agreed, and Julie walked into his life in October 1991.

Julie was a young woman with robust energy, personality, and magnetism. She had been reared in the small Tennessee town of Bolivar, only twenty-two miles southwest of Jackson. When she arrived on the Union campus, she quickly found her place. Soon initiated into the Chi Omega sorority, she also became the sweetheart of Jim McAfee's old fraternity, Sigma Alpha Epsilon. A good student, she was a young lady looking for a bigger world and eager to find her place of contribution and success. Professors and sorority sisters discovered that if you gave Julie a challenge and an assignment, she would accomplish the task with excellence.

Tom discovered this truth as well. Not quite sure how he would supervise this new ball of energy, Tom asked Julie to work in advertising and increase the profitability of the radio station. Soon sales escalated, and Tom could report to Jim that a nearly defunct station was moving into new health.

A few months after their professional relationship began, Julie asked Tom for a favor. Her roommate's wedding was quickly approaching, and Julie was not dating anyone at the time. She asked Tom if he would accompany her to the wedding and the reception party. Tom gladly accepted the invitation, and it was the beginning of a change in their relationship. As Tom remembers, he sat down at his desk one morning and thought, "Oh my gosh! I am now dating an employee!"

Soon after Tom and Julie began dating, Jim and Carolyn visited the Union University campus to attend homecoming festivities and be present for the annual Carolyn Townsend McAfee Organ Concert. Jim and Carolyn invited Tom and Julie to have dinner with them. This was Julie's first introduction to Tom's parents.

A year before, Jim had received an honorary LLD degree from Union University at the 1990 graduation. Julie was aware of this honor and also knew of his reputation as a "successful but tough" businessman. Coming from a middle-class family, Julie also knew that the McAfees were significant contributors to Union University. She was determined that she was not going to be intimidated by Tom's father.

What Jim and Carolyn did not know was that Julie was working with Tom at the radio station. After they met and were eating dinner, it became apparent that Jim was quite smitten with Julie. Playful and full of banter, Jim gave Julie his ultimate compliment, "Young lady, you need to come to work for me!" Julie replied, "Mr. McAfee, I already do. I work in advertising for your radio station." Jim's eyes grew big and then he exclaimed, "Well, I guess that explains why the profits are going up." He was clearly impressed with Julie.

Carolyn and Julie also felt a natural affinity for each other. Julie recalls that Carolyn instantly impressed her as "the epitome of a Southern lady. She was quiet and polite yet warm and affectionate.

We became instant buddies."[14] Tom knew that Julie had the blessing of his parents.

For the next two and a half years, Tom and Julie continued to date. Tom managed the radio station but also enrolled at Union to continue his degree in business. Julie graduated in 1993, while Tom took the "slow track" of a working professional and graduated in 1994. Now the question emerged as to what they would do after graduation?

Tom was now twenty-six-years-old but unsure about his future. He had recently accepted the daunting responsibility of managing all five of the McAfee radio stations spread across Tennessee and Georgia. He sensed that the radio business was rapidly changing and would not continue long-term as one of the McAfee family investments. He suddenly felt adrift at a time when Julie was looking for future direction and relational clarification. Looking deep in his soul, Tom knew that he was not ready to fully commit to engagement and marriage.[15]

Slowly, Tom and Julie drifted apart as Julie returned to Bolivar and Tom contemplated moving back to Georgia. As Tom anticipated, four of the five McAfee owned radio stations were soon sold. Tom personally purchased the remaining station, WNEX in Macon, Georgia, and moved back to the Peach State.

Jim and Carolyn felt grief as Tom and Julie drifted in different directions. Carolyn never removed Julie's name from her address book, and Jim always felt that she hung the moon. But young adults must have freedom to make their choices and move on with life, and the McAfees supported Tom in making the decisions that seemed right for him.[16]

Chapter 12

Transitions and New Beginnings, 1994–1997

From 1987 through 1994, Jim McAfee guided Hallmark Healthcare Corporation to increasing profits, productivity, and institutional health. The key to Jim's success was not good luck; it was a dogged and persistent determination to succeed.

Robert (Bob) Miller is an outstanding attorney who, for many years, was a partner at the prestigious King & Spalding law firm in Atlanta specializing in healthcare law. Jim asked Bob to serve as the legal counsel for National Healthcare as it transitioned into becoming Hallmark Healthcare Corporation. Reflecting on Jim's success with Hallmark, Bob comments: "When Jim first bought National Healthcare it was just a mess. I didn't think Jim could turn National around. But Jim was tenacious. Jim did not have *mean* tenacity. But he had *firm* tenacity. It is real easy to get mean spirited when you are locked in combat with banks over big money. But banks respected Jim. He was not mean spirited. However, he was the most tenacious man I ever knew. And tenacity was the secret to his success."[1]

However, as Jim approached his mid-fifties, he realized that it was time for him to moderate the intensity of his life and create an evolving exit strategy leading to semi-retirement. Like a veteran surfer riding the crest of a magnificent wave, Jim sensed that the ride had peaked for him at Hallmark and another chapter of life was approaching.

In 1994, at age fifty-four, Jim was made a lucrative offer for the purchase of Hallmark Healthcare Systems by Community Hospitals in Nashville. In addition to the cash purchase, Jim was also offered stock in the new merger company. After Jim accepted the offer, both he and Kay Slayden were asked to become members of the board of directors of Community Hospitals in Nashville. Community Hospitals proved to be a profitable investment for Jim, and several years later it was bought by Forstmann Little & Company, one of the largest private equity firms globally. Again, Jim's investments multiplied.[2]

As Jim and Kay received their earnings from the sale of Community Hospitals, Kay talked Jim into one final investment on a much smaller scale; a sure investment Jim could play with while he shifted most of his focus into philanthropic pursuits.

Tenant Healthcare Corporation owned 105 psychiatric hospitals at a time when health insurance companies were growing more restrictive on payments for psychiatric treatment. In addition, Tenant was guilty of fraudulent activity regarding Medicare payment policies. As a result, they were legally mandated to dispose of their hospital holdings within a three-year period of time. The combined value of the distressed hospitals was greatly reduced, and Tenant was running out of time. Jim inspected ten of the best Tenant hospitals and decided to purchase six of them. He quickly sold four for a significant profit, recouped his initial investment, and retained the two best hospitals located in Georgia and Virginia. These two hospitals became part of the final small hospital corporation that Jim founded, Hallmark Systems, Inc., which exists today.[3]

Though Jim would remain as chairman of Hallmark Systems, Inc., he now transitioned to primarily managing the funds within his own substantial McAfee Foundation, as well as increasing his participation on boards and advisory committees of universities, religious organizations, charities, and specific causes that interested him. Jim was also honored by his profession with invitations to serve on the American Hospital Association board of trustees, as well as the board of governors of the Federation of American Health Systems. But above all, it was time for Jim to move into a primarily philanthropic stage of life—a chapter that would entail his greatest contribution, achievement, and legacy.

As Jim made this transition, Tom became increasingly engaged in the family business, receiving valuable experience that would prepare him for the day when he would be responsible for the McAfee Foundation and Hallmark Systems. Though at times Jim could be critical or demanding with co-workers, Jim knew that his son was bright, talented, creative, and could lead the McAfee enterprises into a new day for another generation. In time, Tom would become the executive director of the McAfee Foundation and would work in partnership with his father in the administration of Hallmark Systems.

At the same moment that Jim was transitioning out of the healthcare industry and preparing for semi-retirement, his religious cradle—the Southern Baptist Convention—was increasingly embroiled in controversy. Since 1979, the more conservative wing of Southern Baptists had slowly gained total national control of most boards, agencies, seminaries, and missionary agencies within the denomination. Even most Southern Baptist state conventions had succumbed to this move toward fundamentalism, and the Georgia Baptist Convention was no exception.

Jim and Carolyn's church in Atlanta, Second-Ponce de Leon Baptist Church, had staunchly resisted such denominational encroachment and had remained a moderate church committed to individual freedom and the acceptance of theological diversity. But increasingly, Jim was disturbed by the emerging ultra-conservative theological direction of his denomination. As he told several of his friends, "If it wasn't for Carolyn's commitment, I just might have to become a Presbyterian."[4]

However, bluster aside, Jim wished to remain a committed Baptist and bristled at being told by ultra-conservatives what he must think and do. Though socially and politically Jim was often stridently conservative, when it came to theology and ecclesiology he demanded utmost personal freedom. Jim would soon be compelled to use his business tenacity to defend this freedom.

Four years earlier, in 1990, an important event had quietly transpired in Atlanta that would give exiled Baptists such as Jim and Carolyn McAfee a place to stand and live out their soul freedom. At the 1990 Southern Baptist Convention in New Orleans, the fundamentalist element of the convention was elected to leadership for the eleventh consecutive year. It was a heated and contentious convention, and most moderate Southern Baptists could see that the old convention would never return to a more balanced and cooperative spirit or inclusive nature. Because of this, Dr. Daniel Vestal, the pastor of Tallowood Baptist Church in Houston, Texas, called for a dialogue among moderate Baptists to take place in Atlanta to discuss their future in the Southern Baptist Convention. Two months later, more than three thousand moderate Southern Baptists attended this meeting.

A second dialogue session re-convened in Atlanta a year later, in May 1991, and the attendance doubled to six thousand. The result was an enthusiastic vote to form the Cooperative Baptist Fellowship, which would serve not as a new convention but rather as an independent organization for a displaced Southern Baptist constituency who held moderate, progressive, and ecumenical views. As Daniel Vestal would tell these freedom-loving Baptists, "We're here because we're sensing that God is doing a new thing!"

As a result of this meeting, the Cooperative Baptist Fellowship was born, a constitution written, a budget approved, and a dream of doing worldwide missions spawned. Dr. Cecil Sherman, pastor of the First Baptist Church of Asheville, North Carolina, was elected to be the first Coordinator of the Fellowship, and Atlanta was chosen to be the home of the Cooperative Baptist Fellowship's future offices and staff. A place of freedom for Baptists such as the McAfees had been created in the midst of turmoil and planted in the McAfees' own backyard in Georgia.[5]

In order to communicate and coordinate ministry within Cooperative Baptist Fellowship circles, a strong and effective print media needed to be developed. In 1983, a newspaper for moderate Baptists had been started under the leadership of Walker Knight and named *SBC Today.* Though limited in financial resources and distribution, the paper played an important role. However, the vitality and circulation of the paper was increasingly waning. In 1991, the name of the paper was changed to *Baptists Today*, and a concerted effort was made to extend the reach of the paper to all Baptists around the world. However, the publication continued to be anemic, and by 1997 the newspaper's board of directors was giving serious consideration to ceasing production.

Jim saw a clear need for *Baptists Today* to succeed if moderate and progressive Baptists were to remain united and focused on critical ministry objectives. Urged by prominent Baptist leaders, Jim contacted the paper's board of directors and offered to give personal leadership and a financial contribution to jump start the paper and give it new life.

Eager for McAfee's help and support, a new board was formed in 1998 under Jim's leadership, and he personally committed significant sums to enrich and vitalize the paper. In 1998, the paper was moved from Atlanta to Macon and relocated to the campus of Mercer University. In March 2000, John Pierce was selected to be the new executive editor, and the paper quickly surged into a new chapter of productivity and effectiveness. Reflecting on these days of recovery, Pierce states, "Though *Baptists Today* is a non-profit organization, Jim McAfee always wanted it to be a well-run business. Today, stewardship, legal matters, and accounting are taken very seriously. During the last twelve years the paper has run on a professional business model that Jim McAfee influenced and shaped.

Jim also recruited many lay people as well as influential ministers and denominational leaders to serve on the board. He gave the paper new life and direction."[6]

As a young boy in Jackson, Jim began his business education by rising early every morning and tossing newspapers on his paper route. He never dreamed that fifty years later he would still be involved in the newspaper business. As was his custom, he was fascinated with taking distressed and struggling businesses and breathing new life into them.

During this same period of time, Jim grew closer in friendship with Kirby Godsey, president of Mercer University in Macon. Godsey was a major figure in Southern Baptist life and was strident in his opposition to religious intolerance and to a Southern Baptist form of fundamentalism. Trustees at Mercer supported President Godsey and rallied to resist attempts by the Georgia Baptist Convention to reduce intellectual and academic freedom at Mercer. Jim and Carolyn McAfee applauded Godsey's efforts and were impressed by Mercer's plucky intellectual spirit. In 1993, Dr. Godsey extended an invitation for Jim to join the Mercer University board of trustees, and Jim accepted.

In one of Jim's first trustee meetings in 1994, Dr. Chess Smith, Pastor of First Baptist Church of Tifton, Georgia, brought a formal recommendation from a feasibility committee that Mercer start a new seminary to prepare both men and women for professional ministry. His proposal was enthusiastically affirmed, and Jim's interest was pricked. He clearly saw that a new generation of Baptist ministers had to be educated in an environment that resisted Baptist fundamentalism and promoted freedom of academic inquiry and exploration of personal faith. That night, after the trustee meeting, Jim came home and said to Carolyn, "This new seminary is something we need to be involved in." Carolyn was initially surprised at Jim's excitement but was also in full agreement.[7]

It was at the apex of this historic moment that Dr. Godsey and Jim began to discuss the potential of the proposed seminary and how it might be formed. Jim's entrepreneurial spirit lifted again, and he looked at the creation of a fledgling seminary with the same enthusiasm he felt when structuring new healthcare companies. He was instantly committed to this new venture.

Recalling these days, Kirby Godsey remarked, "As Jim and I continued over time to talk and discuss the potential seminary, I clearly saw that Jim was passionately devoted to historical Baptist principles. He saw the error of the resurgence of fundamentalism within the Southern Baptist Convention. And his negative reaction to this was visceral. I also knew that Jim and Carolyn together as a couple understood emotionally and intellectually the need for a school of theology at Mercer. It must be a school committed to religious intellectual freedom and imbued with respect for religious diversity. I felt that together they understood this more than any other family that I knew."[8]

Soon after the trustee vote to form the Mercer School of Theology, Dr. Godsey began a search for a capable academic leader and exceptional scholar to be the founding dean of the Mercer seminary. His attention soon focused on Dr. Alan Culpepper. Culpepper was the son of Baptist missionaries who had served in China, the Philippines, Chile, and Argentina. A man with a worldwide vision, Culpepper was also perhaps the most internationally recognized Baptist scholar in New Testament studies, specializing in the formation and interpretation of the Gospel of John. For seventeen years Culpepper had served as Professor of New Testament and Associate Dean of the School of Theology at the Southern Baptist Theological Seminary in Louisville, Kentucky. Recently he had returned to his alma mater, Baylor University, as Professor of Religion. Godsey was soon in conversation with Culpepper in Waco, Texas, and persuaded him to leave a secure and prestigious position at Baylor to come to Mercer and start a seminary from scratch. Culpepper had not lost his missionary zeal and enthusiastically accepted the challenge.

After much discussion, the Mercer administration and trustees decided that the new seminary should not be located on Mercer's historic undergraduate campus in Macon but rather on the new and emerging graduate school campus in Atlanta. This metropolitan location would have a number of advantages: it would give the Mercer school of theology more national presence; it would ensure greater availability to a wide range of students; and it would enable the new seminary to form a creative consortium with the Methodists' Candler School of Theology at Emory University and the Presbyterians' Columbia Theological Seminary, all within close proximity to each other. The location was a powerful symbol that the Mercer seminary would produce graduates who were ecumenical in spirit, progressive in thought, and international in vision.

When Culpepper arrived on Mercer's Atlanta campus in July 1995, the seminary consisted primarily of note cards and file folders packed into a single cardboard box in Culpepper's car. Facilities were limited to a few empty rooms in the Davis Building and the Swilley Library. An enthusiastic and visionary President Godsey had promised Culpepper, "We will build a signature building for the seminary on the Atlanta campus." But such a building was far beyond the horizon. Now, a small but competent faculty had to be recruited and the first prospective seminary students convinced to enroll in a new seminary. It was a daunting challenge for Culpepper to undertake.[9]

One year later, forty-four students arrived for the first official day of class in August 1996. During that same year, Jim was asked to serve as chair of the Mercer University trustees. An important melding of spirit, strength, and energy was forging together.

It soon became clear that Mercer University's school of theology would continue to experience rapid growth. The limited space temporarily allotted for the seminary on the Atlanta campus was inadequate, and the funds designated to start the seminary would soon be depleted. President Godsey was hard pressed to raise funds for this important graduate school. A year after settling into his duties of chairing the Mercer trustees, Jim was asked by President Godsey if he and Carolyn would meet him in Atlanta for the purpose of discussing their possible financial support for the school of theology. They welcomed the conversation and met Dr. Godsey and Emily Myers, Senior Vice-President of University Advancement, for a preliminary meeting. Again, Jim was confronted with a start-up business that needed a rapid infusion of capital and structure. Remembering that pivotal day, Dr. Godsey stated, "Emily and I met face to face with Jim and Carolyn and I asked them to consider giving a gift of $10 million to endow a school of theology." It was a bold request.[10]

Jim and Carolyn agreed to consider the school's financial need and to meet again after time for thought and reflection. This was the largest bequest that they had ever considered giving to any institution or purpose. It took them little time to decide to contribute this unprecedented gift to Mercer and to make the sustainability of the seminary possible. As President Godsey would later say, "The McAfees are among the most generous people I have ever worked with. They had the spiritual gift of giving. They had the capacity to see beyond themselves and to engage in genuine stewardship. They were not just philanthropists but people with deep purpose and were character driven. They bought into a vision of a university that had intellectual freedom and independence and could be a keystone for preserving Baptist heritage. Their financial gifts *were advocacy* and they were devoted to the entire university."[11]

Likewise, Emily Myers remembered this momentous day and reflected, "Jim McAfee was one of those rare individuals who saw the impact he could make far beyond his lifetime through gifts to education. He and Carolyn wanted to play a major role in preserving the historic traditions of the Baptist faith, so they helped establish Mercer's school of theology. Graduates will fill pulpits in Baptist churches throughout Georgia and the world because of that visionary gift to education."[12]

On April 4, 1997, Mercer University announced that Jim and Carolyn McAfee had given an endowment gift of $10 million to undergird the new school of theology. Dr. Godsey later requested that the trustees name the new school the James and Carolyn McAfee School of Theology.

Not long after becoming a member of the Mercer University board of trustees, Jim was asked in 1995 to serve on the Union University board of trustees. Prior to 1995, all Union University trustees were required to be official residents of the state of Tennessee. However, in 1994, President Hyran Barefoot requested that a minority percentage of trustees be eligible to be nominated from diverse states. Jim was the first Union trustee to be selected from Georgia, and he would serve from 1995–2001.

During the same year that Jim became a Union University trustee, he was also honored when the Union University School of Business was named the James T. McAfee School of Business Administration. One year later, in May 1996, Dr. Barefoot retired as the president of Union. Barefoot was delighted that Jim had been recognized for his outstanding accomplishments during the final months of his presidential tenure.

Being a trustee at Union University also enabled Jim to visit Jackson more frequently during the final months of his elderly father's waning life. While there had been chronic tensions, as well as deep love, in their relationship, both men had mellowed with age. Jim's father was proud of his son's professional success and personal contribution to Union University. He was astounded that the business school at Union University was now named for the little fellow who drove the imaginary bus when he was three-years-old and who sold used ticket stubs to his playmates. Though JT McAfee had struggled to adequately express to his namesake his blessing, it was undeniable that he loved Jim and was thrilled by the man his son had grown to be.

From Jim's perspective, it was also time to come to peace with his father and to accept the fact that he was indeed worthy of his father's blessing, even if the old man had difficulty transforming affirmation into words. Long ago another son of Tennessee—the national poet laureate Robert Penn Warren—had also returned home to come to peace with his father shortly before his death. Writing years later, Warren recalled gazing at his elderly father sitting in a rocking chair with a blanket draped across his thin body as the thermometer dropped and a harsh winter evening descended. The Tennessee poet scratched out this late night silent monologue:

> Dear Father—Sir —the "Sir" being
> The sometimes disturbed recollection
> Of the time when you were big, and not dead, and I
> Was little, and all boys, of that time and place, automatically
> Said that to their fathers, and to any other grown man,
> White of course, or damned well got their blocks
> Knocked off.
>
> So, Sir, I
> Who certainly could never have addressed you on a matter
> As important as this when you were not dead, now
> Address you on it for the last time, even though
> Not being, after all my previous and sometimes desperate efforts,
> Sure what a son can ever say to a father, even
> A dead one…

... Reality is hard enough to come by, but even
In its absence we need not blaspheme
It.

Not that
You ever could, God knows. Though I,
No doubt, have, and even now
Run the risk of doing so when I say
That I live in a profound, though
Painful, gratitude to you for what
You could not help but be: i.e., yourself.[13]

In 1997, JT McAfee passed away at the age of eighty-nine. He had insisted that his funeral be simple and frugal. Jim and his older brother, Bill, invited Dr. Hyran Barefoot to preside at the funeral service in Jackson and to give the eulogy. Twenty-two years after Frances McAfee was laid to rest, her husband was now reunited with her. Standing by their graves, Jim and Bill knew that they were now the white-haired patriarchs of the McAfee clan. Life had come full circle.[14]

Swallowing hard, Jim looked at the fresh soil on his father's grave and knew the meaning of Robert Penn Warren's words: "I live in a profound, though painful, gratitude to you for what you could not help but be: i.e. yourself." Peace, forgiveness, acceptance, and reunion had come. A father had lived long enough to experience the greatness of his son. A son had matured to embrace and accept the inevitable contradictions and dualities found in every loving human being.

Just as Jim was experiencing the death of his father, Carolyn was also facing the decline and passing away of her parents who had been married and lived together in the same small town of Parsons for sixty-five years. Her mother, Sophia Malin Townsend, lived to age ninety-one and died the same year as JT McAfee. Carolyn's father would continue to live until the age of ninety-eight and passed away in 2001. This was a season of loss for Jim and Carolyn but also a season of gain. For in the passing away of parents there was the increased realization that life leads on to more life and eternity is real. As the American playwright and novelist Thornton Wilder wrote, "We all know that something is *eternal.* And it ain't houses and it ain't names, and it ain't earth, and it ain't even the stars.... Everyone knows in their bones that something is eternal, and that something has to do with human beings."[15]

Chapter 13

Changing Tides, 1998–2004

Approaching his sixtieth birthday, Jim began to reflect on his priorities and his vision for his future. At age forty-seven he had suffered a major heart attack that had severely damaged his heart muscle. Yet over the last decade, he had squeezed more out of life than ever before. Now Jim yearned to live a more balanced life and enjoy the retirement years. But this did not mean that he wanted to sit on the porch and idly watch life pass by. Rather, Jim harkened to a quote attributed to Benjamin Franklin: "There is nothing wrong with retirement as long as it doesn't interfere with your work."

Jim's real question was this: "What is now my truest work in the second half of life?" Jim knew his answer. Both he and Carolyn wanted to focus their energy and resources on many diverse projects and institutions that would positively shape the minds and spirits of future generations. As Emily Myers would later reflect, "Jim wanted to contribute and use his finances and leadership well. He would do whatever necessary to help any group he connected with to be successful. He was willing to be front and center."

In Atlanta, the James and Carolyn McAfee School of Theology was growing and the Cooperative Baptist Fellowship was aggressively expanding its global mission efforts. Both organizations needed newer and larger physical facilities. Shortly before his father's death, Jim and Carolyn contributed additional funds to Mercer University to construct a beautiful new building to house the McAfee School of Theology on the Atlanta campus. When completed, the McAfee School of Theology occupied the first floor of the facility while the Cooperative Baptist Fellowship leased office space on the second floor. The gift of the new building would not only sustain both organizations but would allow young seminary students to work side-by-side with a vital missions program. This one building symbolized the future for an emerging generation of Baptists.[1]

Jim also became involved with the O'More College of Design, a small institution in Nashville that specialized in fashion and interior design. Though this was an unusual venture for him, Jim had always had an aesthetic bent, and he was interested in art, fashion, and the tasteful design and appointment of buildings, houses, and landscapes.

Jim was introduced to O'More College of Design when he was contacted by an old friend, Randall Yearwood. Years before, Yearwood had been the architect who had worked with Jim to design the addition for Jim's first hospital in Coffee County, Tennessee. Now, Yearwood was the president of O'More. Pressed by academic demands, building needs, and the constant stress of financial development, Yearwood wanted to talk to Jim about fiscal development and management. Jim gladly became involved in helping Randall and ultimately was asked to serve on O'More's board of trustees.

Some months later in 1999, Randall Yearwood resigned from O'More, and a young man, Mark Hilliard, became president. Mark was an accomplished artist but was still growing into the role of higher education administration. Jim reached out to Mark and became a mentor, professional advisor, and friend. As Jim grew older, he loved to coach young adults in areas of leadership, vision, and management. O'More College of Design became one of his favorite projects.[2]

Perhaps Jim's most unusual investment harkened back to his childhood love of Lionel trains. When Jim and Carolyn first bought a vacation house in the mountainous environs of Big Canoe, Jim became fascinated with the Georgia Northeastern Railroad. This is a short-line freight railroad that runs from Marietta, Georgia, northwest through the emerging mountains to Blue Ridge, Georgia. Chartered in 1854, the Georgia Northeastern Railroad primarily hauls poultry, chicken feed, grain, timber, and marble products. Its real future potential, however, was to become a commuter rail that would connect resort communities such as Big Canoe to the business world of Atlanta.

Jim Martin, retired president of Auburn University, fondly remembers visits that he and his wife enjoyed with the McAfees at Big Canoe. One Christmas season, Jim purchased large quantities of candy and insisted that Jim Martin accompany him on a Santa Claus trip. Riding on a Georgia Northeastern freight car carrying chicken feed, the two men threw candy to children as they slowly passed by small town stations and railroad crossings. Jim Martin remembers the childlike merriment that exuded from Jim McAfee as they tossed pound after pound of candy to surprised and wild-eyed little kids. It was a journey back into time, replete with fond memories of the 1940s and rural America.

At the end of 1998, Jim completed his first five-year term on the Mercer University board of trustees. Jim had given able leadership as chairperson, supporting President Godsey through denominational turmoil as well as rapid expansion of the university. It was now time to take a rest from these institutional demands and focus more on personal pursuits.

Jim and Carolyn accelerated their plans for travel. Jim particularly enjoyed exploring the British Isles. He had always been a car enthusiast, was intrigued by British automobiles, and was particularly relished the challenge of driving on "the wrong side of the road." Jim and Carolyn loved to rent a car and lose themselves in the British countryside. Jim was especially interested in learning more about the McAfee clan in Scotland, exploring his family history, and savoring the home country. Many weeks were spent in such pursuits and gave Jim an escape from work and responsibility.

Jim and Carolyn also enjoyed designing houses and dabbling in landscape architecture. Several years before, they had sold their first house in Big Canoe and had purchased a new house on one of the highest ridges. Now they began to envision a second retirement house to be built at Seabrook. This would be their final construction project, a unique dream home where they would spend the rest of their lives. As the new millennium approached, they explored undeveloped lots on Seabrook Island and conversed with an architect. They chose a location that was near the ocean, yet was sheltered by sand dunes and shaded by live oaks that had survived the worst of hurricanes. They commissioned an architect to draw the plans and begin construction.

Though Jim had made major changes in his diet following his heart attack, he still loved food and liked to find new restaurants. His favorite restaurant of all time became *Bones* on Piedmont Avenue in Atlanta. Bones was established in 1979 and quickly became known as the finest steak house in the country. Jim became such a regular customer that he made an arrangement with the manager to always sit at the same table. Nothing thrilled Jim more than to hear the maître d' intone, "Mr. McAfee, your table is ready." Many nights were spent with old friends savoring food and fond memories. For Jim, *Bones* was a haven to get away from it all and to drink deeply of the cup of camaraderie and relaxation.

After a two-year hiatus from university governance, Jim was once again invited by Mercer University to serve on their board of trustees from 2000 to 2005. At the same time, Belmont University, a sister Baptist school in Nashville, also asked Jim to be a trustee. Taking a deep breath, Jim accepted both invitations, wanting to remain loyal to Mercer but also desiring to influence Baptist higher education in Tennessee. It was difficult for Jim not to accept positions of leadership and influence when he knew he could make a difference, and he perceived this as an important part of his life's contribution and legacy.

As his parents moved closer to retirement, Tom was also making important changes in his life. The McAfees had left the radio business behind them, and Tom was now working closely with his father. After graduation from Union University in 1994, Tom had moved back to Atlanta and earned a Master of Business Administration degree from Mercer University's Eugene W. Stetson School of Business and Economics. Tom excelled in his studies and found his natural academic niche. He also completed a Financial Planning Certificate at Oglethorpe University, also in Atlanta. Tom now served as Vice-President for Financial Operations with Hallmark Systems, Inc., and managed the family foundation. Tom knew that as Jim moved into full retirement, he would direct their foundation's investments and business ventures. This was a career that both fulfilled and excited Tom.

During the millennium year of 2000, Tom and Julie Crangle rekindled their relationship left behind in college years and began a long-distance courtship between Georgia and western Tennessee. At first the relationship was casual and based more on old friendship than romance. Much of their communication was through emails and phone calls. However, over the next few years, a natural friendship evolved into a serious romantic relationship.

During the fall of 2003, Tom and Julie began to discuss engagement and marriage. Julie traveled to Atlanta to visit with the McAfees, and Jim and Carolyn were thrilled to see her again. They had always loved Julie and were now hopeful that the relationship might lead to marriage. During this visit Tom and Julie walked along the bank of the Chattahoochee River and discussed marriage within the next six months. Returning home, Tom shared with Jim his intentions to marry Julie. Jim looked up with delight on his face and chortled, "Well, it's about time!!" Tom and Julie were engaged to be married on March 6, 2004.

The wedding was in Julie's hometown of Bolivar, Tennessee, at the First Presbyterian Church. The sanctuary is a small and quaint pre-Civil War structure with fifteen rows of pews and a hand-pumped organ. Julie's bouquet was created from daffodils that Tom and Julie picked the day before during a rainstorm in Grandmother Townsend's vast backyard of flowers. It was a simple but elegant wedding, and Dr. Hyran Barefoot once again conducted a McAfee family service. The sanctuary was filled with a profound feeling of completeness and celebration as families gathered, vows were said, and Julie and Tom brought to fulfillment a lifelong commitment that had been kindled a dozen years before during college.[3]

After sending Tom and Julie off on a honeymoon to Hawaii, Jim and Carolyn returned to Atlanta to face an unexpected dilemma. Planning to move permanently to Seabrook, they had placed their Atlanta house on the market. Shortly after the wedding, their house sold and had to be vacated immediately.

In recent months, Tom had been living and working out of *Sea View*—the first house the McAfees had built at Seabrook nineteen years before in 1985. *Sea View* was where Tom intended to bring his bride after their honeymoon and quietly begin their first chapter of marriage. However, with Jim and Carolyn suddenly vacating their house in Atlanta and needing to be frequently in Seabrook to supervise the final construction of their new home, the family decided that both couples would temporarily live together at *Sea View.* Though the house was big and multi-storied, it was not the ideal situation for either couple. This would be a time of adjustment that would require much patience, understanding, and a significant sense of humor.

As Jim and Carolyn were transitioning to Seabrook in July, Jim received the shocking news that his older brother, Bill, had suddenly died of a heart attack. Not only was this loss difficult to bear, it also brought Jim face-to-face with his own mortality again. The same insidious disease of arteriosclerosis had attacked the lives of both brothers, and it was now profoundly clear that this disease could kill.

Returning from Bill's funeral, Jim was overwhelmed not only by grief but also by the disequilibrium of a major household move and the frustration of an unfinished new house. It seemed that everything that could slow the building process did so. Jim's intensity and tenacity were overwhelming him, and he was not making the lives of his contractors easy. The new house was more than six months behind schedule.

For two long and hot summer months, Tom and Julie prayed for patience, Jim kept a cautious eye on his blood pressure, and Carolyn played the marvelous role of peacemaker. The new house was finally completed in September, and Jim and Carolyn were able to move in amidst final touch up work and last minute alterations. There was new hope that life would regain equilibrium and a happy balance.

A month after moving into their lovely new home, Jim and Carolyn were planning to travel to Virginia for a board meeting at the hospital they owned in Richmond. On the way, they stopped for rest and relaxation in Big Canoe. Fall was approaching, Halloween was just around the corner, and it was cool enough in the evenings for a cozy fire in the hearth. Though it was raining and foggy, there was a delightful feeling of snuggling up with a good book and catching up on sleep. The recent pressures at Seabrook faded away into mountain beauty.

However, Jim soon began to feel the symptoms of a bad cold or flu approaching. He felt achy and weak. With Bill's recent death, Carolyn took no chances and called Jim's internist in Atlanta. The internist told Carolyn to drive Jim down to his office and he would give him a quick check-up. Not planning to spend the night, they jumped in the car wearing their walking clothes, hoping to beat rush hour traffic.

On the way to Atlanta, Jim felt worse but he also knew that he had completed an extensive physical examination a few months before and had been declared fit and healthy. What he needed was a good round of antibiotics and an antihistamine. However, on arrival at the doctor's office, he received a battery of blood tests and a routine electrocardiogram. In a few minutes, the doctor walked into Jim's examination room with a concerned look and said, "Jim, these tests show that you have recently had a heart attack and are on the verge of having another one right now. We've got to get you to Piedmont Hospital immediately." Not waiting for an ambulance, they loaded Jim into the car and Carolyn immediately rushed him to the nearby hospital.

As they arrived at the emergency room, a gurney was waiting and Jim received immediate critical care attention. Following multiple tests, it was clear that Jim's coronary arteries were severely blocked and that he would need either cardiovascular stents and angioplasty or more radical coronary artery bypass surgery. After intense debate, the team of cardiologists concluded the only option was bypass surgery. Jim was immediately prepped for surgery. Carolyn called Tom and Julie at Seabrook, and they left for Atlanta.

The surgery was long but successful. Jim received a quadruple bypass and a temporary intra-aortic balloon pump was inserted to help his weakened heart rest and increase cardiac output. When Tom and Julie arrived, Jim was still sedated, and the family received a positive report. Tom then left to drive to Big Canoe to pack some clothes for his mother and bring them back to the hospital.

Exhausted, Tom spent the night at Big Canoe and left early the next morning to return to Atlanta. When he arrived, he was delighted to find Jim awake and in a good mood. Dr. Godsey was visiting, and Jim was drowsily introducing his nurses to Mercer's president. For the next few days, Jim continued to hold court as more and more visitors came by to wish him well. A sense of health was returning.

The arteries were unblocked and Jim could hope for more years of life, creative work, and enjoyment.

The day came when his condition had improved to the point where the balloon pump could be withdrawn from his heart. However, without the pump, Jim's heart soon began to fail. Though the clogged arteries were now open and blood freely flowing, the damaged heart muscle was proving incapable of pumping sufficiently. Jim was immediately sedated and placed on a respirator in the hope that with increased rest, the heart's pumping function might improve. However, each day Jim grew weaker, and he was placed on life support.

On November 2, the consulting doctors met with the McAfee family and Dr. Godsey. The doctors informed them that the prognosis did not look good and that within the next day or two the family would need to decide whether to remove Jim from life support. Mercifully, Jim's heart stopped beating a few hours later and such a traumatic decision was not required.

Carolyn, Tom, and Julie were shattered by grief but not by surprise. They had sensed that the end was near. Yet no one is ever prepared for such finality and shock. Instantly, the family coped by embracing each other and addressing the immediacy of funeral preparations. Mercer's Senior Vice-President, Emily Myers—whom Jim had affectionately nicknamed "The General"—swung into action and helped Carolyn plan the funeral service at Second Ponce de Leon Baptist Church. Tom remembered that Jim had a favorite pair of shoes at Seabrook that he had fondly called "my burying shoes." Tom headed back to Seabrook to pick up dress clothes for the family and his father's special shoes. Carolyn now faced the daunting decision of where Jim's body would be interred. Neither Jim nor Carolyn had wanted to discuss the matter in recent years, seeing such planning as less than positive and optimistic, but the time had now come for a sudden decision. The family chose to bury Jim at Big Canoe and soon departed to select a burial plot.

Numbness and disbelief is the first stage of significant grief and enables families to function through crisis. Carolyn responded with dignity and firm resolve, and with the help of dear friends, discovered that indeed she could "do all things through Christ who strengthens me." In good Tennessee vernacular, "she was a trooper" of the highest order.

Jim's funeral service was truly a worship experience and a time of praise and gratitude. His pastor, Dr. David Sapp, conducted the service and wove together the voices of a number of speakers and musicians into one unified expression of thanksgiving for a life of profound contribution. Dr. John Claypool led in the reading of scripture and prayer. The *Mercer Singers* lifted spirits and harkened faith with renditions of "My Shepherd Will Supply My Need" and "When I Survey the Wondrous Cross." Dr. Hyran Barefoot's familiar voice brought comfort as he read scripture and gave a pastoral prayer. Finally, Dr. Kirby Godsey stood to give the eulogy. Always an elegant and profound speaker, Godsey riveted his audience:

> Jim lived with passion and intensity. He has wrung more from 65 years than most people could in twice the days. It is tempting for us to want him to have done it a little differently—to have run a little slower, to have lowered the wick, but it is foolishness. Jim lived with a high spirit and with convictions that ran deep. Jim lived life with energy and stamina and joy until the end. His heart failed him. His spirit never did!
>
> So, Jim's life should never be measured by the calendar. Nor can ours. Jim's life will be measured by achievement and laughter, by joy and family, by corporate leadership, and by his unbounded spirit of generosity....

> One lesson we can learn from this Christian gentleman is that every person's life is a gift.... So, we would miss the most important lesson in Jim's story unless we are reminded of our own special gifts. You and I, like Jim, stand in a singular, unduplicated place on the stage of human history. Whenever you and I fail to fulfill the promise of our lives, that promise simply remains unfulfilled—forever. So, in our morning of mourning, let us remember that Jim lived life to the limits. He was a special gift, and so are you....
>
> Our highest and most noble tribute to Jim's presence with us will be to embrace life with the profound spirit of faith and hope that enabled him, over and over again, to make a difference.[4]

Inspired by the challenge of Dr. Godsey, Mercer University's Professor of Music and university organist, Dr. Robert Parris, thrilled the congregation as he opened the great pipe organ to full crescendo and led the congregation in a concluding hymn, "To God Be the Glory," followed by the benediction by Dr. Alan Culpepper, dean of the McAfee School of Theology. As family and friends sat transfixed, Dr. Parris transitioned into the organ postlude and played Jim's favorite organ composition, Widor's exultant *Toccata.* The triumphant strains of the organ postlude concluded a memorable hour of worship and praise for a life that was lived to the hilt. Friends, colleagues, and family members left with the firm resolve "to make a difference." Jim would have designed the service no other way.

Quietly, the family and a few close friends departed for the solace of Big Canoe. The next morning, amidst the beauty of north Georgia mountains, Jim was laid to rest. There was no pipe organ. No bagpipe from Scotland. There need not be. The simple and profound quietness embraced the weary, and the words of the psalmist lifted their eyes to the hills from whence their help would come.[5]

Dr. Jimmy Allen, chaplain of Big Canoe Chapel, reflected on how death is like moving from one house to another; the same life lived in many places. Then, across the centuries the words of the old Quaker, William Penn, softly whispered, "We give back to you, O God, those whom you gave to us. You did not lose them when you gave them to us, and we do not lose them by their return to you. Your dear Son has taught us that life is eternal and love cannot die. So death is only a horizon and a horizon is only the limit of our sight."[6]

Chapter 14

The Story Continues

It has been ten years since Jim McAfee was laid to rest in Big Canoe, Georgia, but much of importance has transpired in those years as the story of the McAfee family has continued to unfold.

Shortly before Jim's first heart attack in 1987, Jim and Carolyn created the James T. McAfee, Jr., and Carolyn T. McAfee Foundation. By the time of Jim's death seventeen years later, the McAfee Foundation had grown exponentially and was a significant source of support and benevolence for many worthy and philanthropic pursuits.

At the time of Jim's death in 2004, Tom McAfee had worked with his father for fourteen years. Beginning in 1990, when he was twenty-two years old, Tom managed the McAfee radio stations in Jackson, Tennessee, and Macon, Georgia. When the McAfees sold their radio business, Tom moved back to Atlanta in 1998 to work with the McAfee Foundation. Tom also began an aggressive educational pursuit to prepare for this new responsibility.

Tom now laughs and quips that he earned a doctorate—summa cum laude—from the "Jim McAfee School of Business Management." Tom did indeed learn much from his father, but he also earned a master's degree in Business Administration from the Stetson School of Business at Mercer University as well as a Certification in Financial Planning from Oglethorpe University. With both academic and practical preparation, Tom was soon poised to assume significant leadership.

In 1998, Tom became the full-time executive director of the McAfee Foundation. Jim and Tom related well professionally, and

Tom remembers these years of collaboration as being "a happy experience with a sense of joy and mutual appreciation for each other." Tom also recalls that his father was "preparing me for what I needed to know whether I appreciated it, or understood it, or not. I soon learned 'the ins and outs' of the Jim McAfee philosophy of business."[1]

In 2001, three years prior to Jim's sudden death, Tom began to assume the responsibility of leadership for not only the McAfee Foundation, but also for Jim's final hospital business venture, Hallmark Systems. At the time, Hallmark Systems owned four hospitals, and Tom was given the responsibility of rehabilitating several of these properties and selling them. Tom was successful in doing so, and Hallmark Systems ultimately retained two of the hospital properties. The result of Tom and Jim's collaboration was that by the time of Jim's death in 2004, Hallmark Systems had no debt, owned two profitable hospitals, and the McAfee Foundation was in excellent financial health, actively supporting a number of grants, primarily in the fields of higher education and the fine arts.

Upon Jim's death in 2004, the board of directors at Hallmark Systems elected Tom as the chairman and president of Hallmark Systems, and he also continued his work as the executive director of the McAfee Foundation. Tom was thirty-six years old and had suddenly been thrust into a position of major financial and corporate responsibility. When asked how he felt during these initial days of executive leadership, Tom replied, "Well, it was a lot of responsibility in an industry I didn't fully understand or ever dreamed of being ultimately responsible for. However, I have continued to serve until this day with a great board of directors who are veterans of major corporate leadership. They have given me guidance and support and encouragement. Today, I am very happy and fulfilled in my professional work, and it is a great organization that I am honored to lead."

Carolyn was also placed in a position of greater responsibility and leadership in the McAfee business world. Always a supporting partner and prominent advisor in all that Jim did, she nevertheless now joined Tom in providing leadership to both the McAfee Foundation and Hallmark Systems.

Remembering this time of sudden grief and enormous responsibility, Carolyn reflected, "There were days after Jim's funeral when I did not even know how to sort the mail. Taxes were coming in. I was still trying to get the new house construction completed at Seabrook and so grief stricken that Jim had only been able to live in the house for six weeks. But you learn to do what you have to do!"

Slowly, equilibrium returned to the McAfee family, and their business ventures remained stable and healthy. When reflecting on what he learned most from his father about business management, Tom observed, "Dad had two guiding principles. First, always have the confidence and wisdom to surround yourself with people who are better than you are and who have knowledge in areas outside of your expertise. And, second, always be honest and have integrity. As simple as this seems, it is the essence of good business management."

For the last ten years, Tom and Carolyn have continued to live by these principles. But most important, Tom has discovered what Jim meant when he frequently said, "Good business is great fun!" Helping others through generous philanthropy while wisely preserving and expanding investments has continued to create for the McAfees a rewarding sense of personal mission and contribution.

Following Jim's death, both Carolyn and Tom served on Mercer University's board of trustees. During the academic year of 2005, Mercer experienced a significant moment in its long history. It occurred during a time of crisis that engendered both danger and opportunity. As the Georgia Baptist Convention continued to become more conservative and restrictive with regard to its perspective on theological and academic freedom, increasing tensions arose between the Convention and Mercer University. It became clear to both parties that Mercer should become an independent and freestanding university. In November 2005, the Georgia Baptist Convention officially voted to sever ties with Mercer University.

At the time of severance, Dr. Kirby Godsey had served as Mercer's president for twenty-six productive years, longer than any other president, and had already announced his impending retirement, effective June 30, 2006. Dr. Godsey knew that the next Mercer board of trustees meeting in December 2005 would be historic, transitional, and come at a critical time with regard to achieving a promising future. Godsey requested that this meeting be held not on the Mercer campus in Macon, Georgia, but rather in the small village of Penfield, Georgia, the historic site of Mercer's initial founding in 1833. William D. Underwood, the future president of Mercer, was also invited to attend this board meeting to be introduced to the Mercer board of trustees. It was, indeed, a propitious moment.

As the trustees gathered during the season of Advent in the old Penfield Baptist Church, both Tom and Carolyn were in attendance. Carolyn recalls that, "Dr. Godsey gave a beautiful lesson about the founding of Mercer at Penfield and our history and heritage. Afterwards, we went to the cemetery and laid wreaths on Jesse Mercer's grave, as well as the graves of other prominent Mercer professors and leaders. Just standing there was an awesome experience."

Independently of each other, Carolyn, Tom, and his wife, Julie, quietly imagined that this beautiful, quaint, and historic graveyard would be the perfect place for Jim McAfee to be permanently interred. While his burial site in Big Canoe, Georgia, was a place close to Jim's heart, it would be fitting for Jim to be placed in the midst of other men and women who had given so generously and who had sacrificed so much for Mercer University. It was a spontaneous thought born from the beauty, quiet, and solace of a reflective winter afternoon.

Several days later, Tom and Julie mentioned the idea to Carolyn and were delighted that she, too, had shared the same inspiration and dream. A few months later, during a visit by President Godsey to Seabrook Island, Tom discussed the possibility of moving Jim's grave from Big Canoe to Penfield. Dr. Godsey enthusiastically concurred and gave his blessing. Prior to his retirement in June 2006, Dr. Godsey presided over a short graveside service, attended by the McAfee family and a few close friends, as Jim's body was brought to its final resting place. Years later, Carolyn quietly reflected, "This gave to us all a sense of closure. There was a sense of coming home, of belonging, and of purpose."[2]

As Carolyn began the long and difficult process of walking from the darkness of grief back into the sunlight of a new chapter of life, she remembered recent discussions with Jim concerning the importance of perpetuating quality church music. They both felt strongly that a sacred music component should be added to the curriculum of the McAfee School of Theology. In 2005, Carolyn and Tom led the development of the Townsend-McAfee Institute for Church Music, a collaborative venture between the McAfee School of Theology in Atlanta and the Department of Music at the Mercer College of Liberal Arts in Macon. The Institute was named in honor of Carolyn's parents, Raymond and Sophia Townsend. Carolyn's inheritance from her deceased parents formed the seed money that created the fund to start the Institute.

However, as these plans for the Institute for Church Music moved rapidly toward fruition, Carolyn and Tom significantly broadened the scope of their vision and dreams. They both became convinced that the time had come in the life of Mercer University to move the undergraduate Department of Music out of the limited venue at the College of Liberal Arts and to establish a new and separate College of Music that would achieve international recognition. Quietly resolving to provide the founding corpus for the endowment of such a professional college, Tom telephoned President Godsey to ask if they could meet to discuss the possible creation of a College of Music. Dr. Godsey was driving his car when he received Tom's call and almost had a wreck while celebrating this momentous possibility and financial offer.

The Mercer trustees enthusiastically ratified Dr. Godsey's subsequent proposal, and the Townsend School of Music was formed in 2006 and housed in the new Allan and Rosemary McCorkle Music Building, a state-of-the-art facility on the Macon campus. Mercer University became nationally renowned for music, and the Institute of Church Music was at the heart and core of this endeavor. A vision was realized and a dream achieved. And Carolyn McAfee, a young woman who once aspired to be a professor of organ music, had now enabled an excellent school of music to be born.[3]

When the Townsend School of Music opened its doors on July 1, 2006, the McAfee family was in the midst of another major transition. Since 2004, Tom and Julie had lived on Seabrook Island, South Carolina. Carolyn was also living on Seabrook in the new house that she and Jim had designed and had occupied for only a few short weeks before Jim's death. Though the lush island seemed a Garden of Eden, it was isolated and would not be an easy place to raise a future generation of McAfee children. Soon, Tom, Julie, and Carolyn decided that Seabrook was a wonderful place for a vacation, but not a good place for an active professional life. They decided to retain their Seabrook homes for frequent relaxation, but they would return to Macon, Georgia, as a place of permanent residence.

Carolyn soon found a house in Macon that she liked, and she renovated it to fit her needs. Tom and Julie built a house and dreamed of starting a family. The McAfees were back in Macon by the fall of 2006 and rejoiced their return to a place that felt like home! It was a time of new beginnings and a fresh start for Carolyn. It was the first house that she had not shared with Jim.

As the McAfee family continued to reflect on Jim's life and legacy, they created a significant annual scholarship in 2006 at Mercer University for a junior, senior, or graduate student who exhibits key qualities that Jim McAfee believed were essential to a successful life. Instead of the scholarship being focused on academic achievement, the scholarship is awarded to students who have shown exceptional leadership and service towards others. In the concept documents, it is stated that, "The McAfee Vision and Leadership scholarship recipient will be someone whose life story exhibits willingness to take risks and step outside the academic realm to excel in another way—to make a difference in the lives of others. This person could have a 'C' grade-point average, but if they employ creativity, even at the risk of personal failure, and take real steps toward the improvement of others, they are a prime candidate. Creativity and vision are important, but the ability to translate their passion into action is what separates dreamers from doers."[4]

These qualities were clearly seen in Jim McAfee when he was a college student. Later, these same characteristics led Jim to not only be financially successful, but to also risk and expend his monetary resources to enable others to succeed through education and servant leadership.

Each year at the commencement ceremony at Mercer University, the James T. McAfee, Jr., Endowed Vision and Leadership Scholarship is presented to a worthy student. It is a cogent reminder that excellent academic performance is not as important as a life of sacrificial leadership and service.

Only a few short weeks after moving to Macon, Carolyn visited her doctor in Atlanta for an annual physical. It was the beginning of the Christmas season, and Tom and Julie were expecting their first child. In the midst of Advent expectation, Carolyn received a call from her doctor saying that he wanted to run a few more tests. It was soon confirmed that she had breast cancer. Carolyn had no overt symptoms, but surgery would soon be necessary.

Remembering those moments of surprise and terror, Carolyn recalls that "I was thinking that life was finally about to get back to normal and hoping that things were going to be stable and happy again. And, boom! Like a bolt of lightning I was struck with the realization that I am mortal! Life can change so quickly!"

Carolyn immediately had surgery, which was followed by chemotherapy and radiation, and for the last seven years she has been cancer free. However, this brush with mortality has greatly influenced her perspective. Carolyn now realizes that:

> My cancer experience has made me more aware of the preciousness of life and what I really want to do. I have a deeper understanding of how important life is. I have become more appreciative of my family. I also feel an urgency to define what I want to do and not wait around forever. I want to travel, to be exposed to different cultures and natural beauty, and to take full advantage of educational opportunities. I want to be fully alive in the years that are my gift to live.

The day after Carolyn finished her last radiation treatment, Caroline Zoe McAfee was born to Julie and Tom on June 25, 2007. The sound of her small infant voice heralded new life, a new generation, and an even greater reason to live life to the fullest. Three years later, Mary Malin McAfee was born on May 16, 2009. In twenty short months, Carolyn's life had radically changed, and a grandmother's enthusiasm had brought vibrant health and a new perspective. And, somewhere in heaven, Jim McAfee was beaming brightly. Time had come full circle, and death had been trumped by life.

As Tom and Julie welcomed these precious children into their family, Tom also had the unexpected experience of envisioning a new dream and vocational chapter in his life, and it happened in a most unexpected way.

Hymns have always played a significant role in the McAfee family. Not only was Carolyn an excellent church organist, but Jim had also loved to play hymns on the Hammond organ he had bought Carolyn in the first years of their marriage. One of Tom's vivid memories of childhood was watching Jim play hymns "until the pictures rattled on the walls throughout the house and Dad's face radiated wonder and joy!"

One night, while Tom was at Big Canoe preparing their vacation home for winter weather, he had a vision as he dozed off to sleep. In this vision, he saw a new hymnal being developed by a group of musicians and placed in churches. He woke up with the conviction that what he had seen was more than a dream. It was an exciting and enticing mandate to create a new interdenominational hymnal to invigorate worship and celebrate the Christian year. This thought excited Tom, and he was motivated and filled with creative passion. He knew that he had to act on this new conviction.

Tom soon shared his dream with close friends, who encouraged him to pursue this venture. He quickly assembled an editorial team, which was initially composed of John Simons, Stanley Roberts, Milburn Price, and David Music. Soon, the editorial team had recruited more than fifty other musicians, scholars, and laity from across the continent to serve on committees to design and oversee the hymnal. Tom and Mark Edwards, who had recently retired as minister of music at First Baptist Church in Nashville, Tennessee, went across the country conducting "HymnPosiums," which were listening sessions that allowed church musicians from multiple denominations to express their thoughts as to what was needed to enhance worship services. Slowly, they were able to discern what these diverse churches wanted in a new hymnal. The hymnal was titled *Celebrating Grace*.

After four years of study, design, and production, the *Celebrating Grace Hymnal* premiered at Second-Ponce de Leon Baptist Church in Atlanta on March 8 and 9, 2010. Today, the hymnal is in its eighth printing, and more than 125,000 copies are in circulation. It is quickly becoming a popular Christian hymnal, uniting a broad panorama of Christian churches in the worship of God. This creative venture led Tom into new realms of business and promotion, expanding the McAfee business entrepreneurship and creativity and breathing new life into Tom's soul.

Today, ten years after the death of Jim McAfee, Carolyn, Tom, and Julie have "seized the day" and live busy lives full of service, contributions, and joy. They have continued to follow the family motto of "I want to make difference!" Today, they honor Jim by continuing to expand the family legacy. And, each in their own way, have also lived freely with regard to making individual contributions and offering unique expressions of creativity. The story continues through new generations and into the beckoning future.

Chapter 15

Reflections on the Life-Dream of James T. McAfee, Jr.

This biography of Jim McAfee is being published on the tenth anniversary of his death. Time moves quickly, but his smile still gleams in the memories of many. Though his story is now told, it is also time to reflect briefly on the major themes of this good man's legacy. What can we, the living, learn from this story of a life of contribution and generosity? What was the essence of Jim's character and vision? To aid in such a brief analysis, it is helpful to consider a few thoughts from the work of the adult development theorist, Daniel Levinson.

In Daniel Levinson's seminal work, *The Seasons of a Man's Life,* he posits that the most pervasive dynamic that unifies and invigorates a person's life is the quest to envision, define, and actualize what Levinson calls a dream or life-dream. This life-dream is as unique as our individual DNA, and it begins to evolve in early childhood and continues to grow—and becomes increasingly defined—throughout adulthood. By analyzing and understanding our life-dreams, we are better able to experience and fulfill the deepest desires within us.[1]

A life-dream is composed of at least four component parts: vocation, core beliefs, relationships, and avocation. In order to understand the life-dream and contributions of Jim McAfee, we will briefly analyze and reflect on the four component parts of his dream.

Vocation

It is clear that the focus of Jim's vocational calling emerged quite early in his life. His selling used ticket stubs to his fellow toddlers to ride his imaginary tricycle transit bus reveals a child with a creative imagination and a desire for business. Later an elementary school student riding his bike through the pre-dawn hours and delivering newspapers shows a disciplined young boy who loved to work, a boy who saved his money for a dream car and envisioned a home that he might someday purchase. In high school and college Jim found that working multiple jobs was not something he dreaded or resented, but rather it was an experience that led him to happiness, as he felt mature and fully alive.

From his earliest years, Jim was a natural-born business person and entrepreneur, and he loved the challenge of hard work and long hours of labor. Business and industry were as compelling and alluring to Jim as playing competitive sports was to many of his peers. Jim grasped this gift for business and embraced it as his own greatest talent, and he never looked back.

Marcus Buckingham and Donald Clifton wrote an important book that Jim would have loved. In *Now, Discover Your Strengths,* the authors analyzed a Gallup study that was administered to more than two million people. What they discovered can serve as a much-needed corrective to the American business and education systems. Jim would have bought and given away dozens of copies of this book.[2]

In summation, Buckingham and Clifton contend that education and business are primarily focused on attempting to strengthen people's weaknesses rather than on helping these same people to discover their truest strengths. For example, during college, many budding pre-medical students are beaten down and discouraged by the growing awareness that they are not naturally gifted in chemistry, biology, and physics. They are highly intelligent and compassionate and they love people and have keen relational skills, but science is not their forte. During this academic struggle, they are given little help in discovering what their greatest strengths are, even if these have been evident since early childhood. Higher education and business pursuits often beat people senseless by focusing on their weaknesses.

In contrast to this, Buckingham and Clifton suggest that:

> This is probably what school should be like: a focused hunt for a child's areas of greatest potential. This is probably what work should be like: an intentional effort to find out how each employee might approach world-class performance levels. Unfortunately, neither school nor work seems up to the task. Both are so preoccupied with transferring knowledge and plugging skill gaps that developing awareness of natural talents is disregarded. And so the burden falls on you, the individual. You must lead the search for your talents....Identify your most powerful talents, hone them with skills and knowledge, and you will be well on your way to living the strong life.[3]

Jim "lived the strong life" and did exactly this; he found the courage to be his most true self. From childhood, Jim instinctively knew that business and entrepreneurship were at the core of his being, and when he announced to his fraternity brothers at his college graduation that he had no desire to graduate summa cum laude but rather was ready "to get the hell out of here," he was saying that "My time has come to engage business and industry. This is my talent. This is my passion and longing. This is worthy of my life and my labor!"

Jim's life-long focus on his natural talents led him to the pinnacle of business success and gave him the ability to make a difference in the matters that were the most important to him. Jim's vocational dream to do well in business was one of the four foundations of his life. It was his true calling. Jim would say to young adults today, "Have the courage to live out your most natural and enjoyable talents and strengths."

Core Beliefs

As a person begins to follow their true life-dream, their core beliefs and ethical convictions become the chart and compass that direct their life. Such core beliefs are not only what we profess intellectually, but also what we embrace with our heart and passion. Jim had at least five core beliefs that guided his life and actions.

Christian Faith and Ethics

As this book reveals, when Jim entered adolescence and young adulthood, he was all boy and anything but pious. He loved his fun and could have a good time with the best of his SAE fraternity brothers. Jim could also be critical—and often was—of the life and behavior of the organized Christian church, whether Baptist, Methodist, Presbyterian, Episcopal, Catholic, or Pentecostal. However, Jim's Christian faith had a deep and formative impact with regard to shaping his life-dream.

Jim did not desire to be a successful entrepreneur simply to make money. Rather, he and Carolyn increasingly wanted to use their financial gains to help other people and to help shape and influence the generations that would emerge long after they were dead.

Sitting through many long and droning Baptist sermons, Jim learned the essence of the Golden Rule and sought to treat others with fairness, integrity, and generosity. He also knew that Jesus once said that there were only two ethical mandates that should govern our lives. First, to love and honor God with all that we are and all that we possess. And, second, to love our neighbor as much as we love ourselves. As a married couple, Jim and Carolyn sought to live by these teachings of Jesus as their life-dream evolved.[4]

In particular, they sought to do so by influencing higher education at Belmont University, Mercer University, Rhodes College, and Union University. They wanted to enable and shape a future generation of leaders, musicians, artists, entrepreneurs, and scholars. They gave generously, sacrificially, and with great joy.

It is not possible to understand Jim if you cannot understand his Christian perspective and heritage. Christian ethics formed the foundation of his core beliefs.

The Desire to Make a Difference

Running deeply within the soul of Jim and Carolyn McAfee was the desire to make a difference. This dominant theme emerged early in their marriage. When Carolyn reflected on the days when two cups of coffee and a dozen donuts was a major splurge for the McAfees, her memory was crystal clear that central to their youthful idealism was the quest to make a difference with their lives.

Years later, when they had achieved business success, they better understood how they could make a difference. Growing older, facing health crises, glimpsing the shadow of mortality, and coming to know the fleetingness of time causes one to ask, "What kind of legacy do I want to leave for my children, grandchildren, friends, and people I will never meet? What will be the major themes that define my life?"

Jim and Carolyn did not want to be remembered simply as a married couple that worked hard and achieved success in business. Rather, they wanted to teach by example that the blessing of wealth could be used to help future generations learn, explore, create, achieve, and reach their fullest potential. It was this quest that led the McAfees to generously and with great sacrifice support higher education. They wanted to encourage and shape hundreds of gifted musicians, leaders, entrepreneurs, and ministers. This was what they desired their legacy to reflect. Their contribution and legacy would make a difference that rippled across centuries and generations.

The author Steve Saint once reflected, "Your story is the greatest legacy that you will leave to your friends. It's the longest-lasting legacy you will leave to your heirs."[5] Generations of McAfees and their friends will remember the indelible picture of Jim and Carolyn as newlyweds, sitting in a donut shop and carefully counting their change, silently dreaming of making a difference in their world. This was a core belief. This is their legacy.

Healing the Sick

Both Jim and his brother, Bill, were aware at an early age that healing disease and sickness was central to the ministry of Jesus. Bill was skilled in science and became a physician. Jim recognized his own talent in business, but he struggled to find a type of business that would be worthy of the cost of his life. As Jim neared graduation from Union University, he discovered that hospital administration was a way to combine business and healing. Managing a hospital effectively was as important as being a surgeon or an internist.

For the rest of his life, Jim was involved in healing the sick and comforting those in distress. Slowly, he emerged as a national leader in hospital management. Though the business aspects of his vocation often removed him from the immediacy of personal involvement with the sick, Jim was keenly aware that the governance and policy decisions that he made each day affected individuals, whether a heart patient or a small child struggling to breathe. Jim was passionate about the real purpose of his business ventures, as bringing comfort and healing to others was one of his core beliefs.

Hard Work and Intensity

To know Jim was to observe hard work and experience personal intensity. Jim had deep respect for those who possessed a strong work ethic and a desire to get it done and do it right. Jim could be a taskmaster, but he pushed himself harder than anyone else. He led by example. Being industrious was a core belief.

Jim's intensity was not usually dour or grim. He seldom lost his sense of humor, his abounding wit, or the twinkle in his eyes, as he guided others through encouragement and challenge. However, those same eyes could flash in anger when a job was not done professionally, when laziness was apparent, or when a colleague did not exhibit maturity or responsibility. Jim did not tolerate underperformance.

As with most people, strengths can also be weaknesses. Jim's strong work ethic and personal intensity adversely affected his health. Though his encroaching heart disease was primarily the result of heredity and chemistry, it was also aggravated by the long hours of work and his unrelenting drive to achieve his professional goals. The struggle for a healthy balance is life long for every man and woman—and Jim was no exception—but hard and productive work was clearly one of Jim's greatest joys and deepest core beliefs. His willingness to work and his intensity were the hammer and chisel that shaped his life and helped him craft his contributions and his legacy.

Wise Generosity

As Jim reflected on his own family history and legacy, he knew that a deep and abiding generosity was at the heart of his inter-generational story. As has been told, two of Jim's grandfathers owned country stores in the midst of the Great Depression. Both men were so concerned about the plight of their starving neighbors that they over-extended credit and literally gave their stores away. Forced into bankruptcy, his Grandfather McAfee and Grandfather Hilliard closed their stores, but they continued to care for the poor.

Decades later, as they realized financial success, Jim and Carolyn embraced the family trait of generosity, but they were also determined to be good stewards and to manage their financial resources well. Jim was a businessman who was willing to take risks when appropriate, but he did not take unwise chances or give the store away. He developed a core belief that combined benevolent and sacrificial giving with prudent and wise business management. The result is that the McAfee Foundation has continued to increase in benevolence while maintaining financial strength and integrity.

Relationships

It is true that happiness is primarily created and sustained by the depth and quality of personal relationships. Vocational success without relational depth is empty. Jim's greatest wealth was not measured in money and profit but in warm and meaningful relationships. His relationships were multi-faceted.

Family

In preparation of writing this biography, dozens of interviews were conducted with men and women who knew Jim intimately and worked with him closely. One dominant theme that was stressed was that Jim was a family man. He loved Carolyn, Tom, and Julie deeply. He was also committed to supporting the well being of his large extended family. Jim valued Carolyn's relatives as much as his own McAfee clan. For Jim, blood ran deep.

George Shaunnessey and Jim McAfee worked and traveled together for more than seventeen years. They knew each other well and shared deep mutual respect. When asked about Jim's highest values, George instantly replied, "Jim was one hell of a family man! For Jim, family was first and foremost."[6]

Likewise, Bill Fickling, the founder and president of the Charter Medical Corporation in Macon, Georgia, did not hesitate when asked a similar question: "Jim was a family man. He loved Carolyn and was devoted to her. Occasionally you find a couple that become one entity. Jim and Carolyn did."[7]

Jim was often obsessed by his work and labored long and hard hours. It was a struggle to balance work and family, but it was clear that the focus of his life-dream centered on Carolyn, Tom, and Julie McAfee.

Friendship

As a little boy, Jim was a child who wanted to be constantly surrounded by friends. His friendship with Matt Tomlin began in elementary school and extended until Jim's death. They were playmates, attended the same church, double-dated as teenagers, were classmates at Union University, and later served together as trustees at their alma mater. In characterizing Jim's desire for faithful friendship, Matt remarked, "One thing about Jim's character was that when he became wealthy, it really didn't change him any. He kept in touch with his old friends and the people he grew up with. He always knew where we all were."[8]

One of Jim's closest adult friends was Dr. Kirby Godsey, chancellor of Mercer University. Dr. Godsey reflected that, "Jim was the kind of person that collected friends and maintained them over a long time. Friendship was not situational but lifelong. Jim did not 'move on' but kept friendships alive."[9]

When Tom recalls his childhood, he remembers that his father kept the telephone wires hot by staying in touch with friends from every chapter of his life. Tom reflected, "Once you were his friend, you were his friend. He kept up with you. He spent a lot of time talking to high school and college friends. Those who were successful and those who were not as fortunate. His circle of friends was non-judgmental. And, it was a large circle of friends!"[10]

The one thing that Jim expected of friendship was loyalty. He did not tolerate fair-weather friends, and his anger could flare when someone turned their back or was fickle. For Jim, friendship should be constant and dependable.

Jim often showed particular kindness to friends who had made honest mistakes or had crumpled under the pressure of life. Julie McAfee recalled a moment early in her marriage to Tom when they attended a dinner with her new in-laws. She watched in amazement as "Jim put together a supper table of people who did not know each other but needed each other. He particularly reached out to a pastor who had recently resigned from his church and was quietly and awkwardly visiting that evening. Jim purposefully sat beside him and by his presence let him know that he supported him. I was deeply moved as a young bride and daughter-in-law."[11]

Friendship was second only to family, and Jim's relational world revolved around loyal and consistent friends. As his old fraternity brother, Nathan Pillow, recalled, "Mac would stand by you!"[12]

Mentors

There is a rare and valuable person who sometimes enters the life of fortunate young adults called a mentor. Usually a mentor is an older adult who serves as a role model, supervisor, or teacher and who takes a special interest in a younger colleague. The mentor helps the young adult understand their profession, perfect their craft, and advance within their professional world. Most of all, a mentor is a source of encouragement and blessing. It requires a special person to be a good mentor, and it requires an equally capable and secure young adult to allow a mentor to provide guidance. Jim was blessed with quality mentors.

When Jim completed his course work in hospital administration at Georgia State University, his first supervisor was Bob Jeffries, a first-rate hospital administrator. Bob was a great mentor, and Jim had the humility and wisdom to accept his mentorship. The result was a warm friendship that spanned years.[13]

Later, in his mid-thirties, Jim would meet his primary mentor, Jack Anderson, president of Hospital Affiliates in Nashville,

Tennessee, and a giant in the evolving and massive corporate hospital world. Jack taught Jim how to grow from being the hospital administrator for one hospital to a corporate executive overseeing many hospitals.

What allowed Jim to blossom under these capable mentors was not only the strength of the mentor but the relational trust and openness of Jim McAfee. Family, friends, and mentors were at the center of Jim's relational world.

Employees

Finally, employees played a significant role in Jim's life. Part of Jim's life-dream was to strengthen and help every employee to see a brighter vision and to enable them to achieve their dreams.

Calvin Harrell is now advanced in age. Though his vision is impaired, he recently wrote a letter to Carolyn in which he recalled his days working as an employee in the small Tennessee hospitals where Jim first learned his administrative craft. Mr. Harrell penned these lines:

> The one word to describe Mr. McAfee was honesty. He was my mentor. One night he came by my house and knocked on my kitchen door. He asked me to be in charge of material management at the hospital. Prior to that I had always just worked in the laboratory. I told him I couldn't do it. He said to me, "You have the ability to do anything and you're honest." So, I told him I would do it. Had I not had Jim's example and leadership, I might have been tempted to compromise. But he encouraged me. I could see a reflection of Jesus in this man. He gave to others. And I'm so glad that our paths crossed.[14]

Jim not only learned from his own mentors, but he was also a mentor himself to hundreds of people who were glad that their paths crossed.

Avocation

The last of the four aspects of a life-dream is avocation. Avocation relates to those natural desires in a person's life that may not directly relate to vocation but that are equally as important. Jim's life-dream was enriched and enlarged by many avocational pursuits. A few examples should be mentioned.

A Love of the Horseless Carriage

As a little boy, Jim was fascinated with cars. This attraction never left him. While he did not become a car collector, he did take pride in his automobiles and was excited to see the new models produced each year. As a young adult, Jim simply wanted to own a standard Oldsmobile. While he never yearned to purchase a Rolls Royce, even when he could later afford one, he always admired the sleek lines of well-designed cars. At the time of his death, Jim's pride and joy was a black Jaguar that he drove to work each day. A good automobile was always a pleasant companion in Jim's life. The Jaguar is still parked in Carolyn's garage; it is a member of the family.

Passion for Music

The radio was usually turned on in Jim's car, as he loved music. His mother made sure that young Jim took piano lessons and sang in children's choirs. Jim loved many forms of music, including sacred, choral, classical, jazz, big band, and even rock and roll. Regardless of genre, however, Jim's deepest appreciation was for excellent and well-performed music.

One of the most vital sources of intimacy in Jim and Carolyn's marriage was their shared love of music. Jim's pride in Carolyn's musical ability was obvious and palpable. He beamed when Carolyn played the organ or piano. Music was a special expression of their love for each other, and it was a bond that grew stronger with age.

Later in life, when Jim and Carolyn first considered contributing financially to higher education, their primary focus was usually on music. Their shared love of music shaped their vocation and relationships and expressed the deepest level of their core beliefs.

Travel

Woven throughout the McAfee's married life was an enjoyment of travel. Being reared primarily in the state of Tennessee, they longed to discover a wider world, and this longing grew during their years of marriage. They also wanted their son, Tom, to gain invaluable insights through travel. Business trips and summer vacations were often planned around journeys to new places. Some of Tom's fondest childhood memories were of these vacation weeks.

Later, the McAfees ventured outside the United States and fell in love with Great Britain. Jim particularly enjoyed the discovery of his Scottish heritage. He wanted to visit every site where he had discovered that a McAfee ancestor had lived. Aggressively driving British cars, he learned to drive on the wrong side of the road and shift gears with his left hand. Jim felt vital and alive in the Scottish Highlands.

Following Jim's death, Carolyn continued to take frequent international trips. Recently, during her first exploration of Southeast Asia, she was enthralled with the beauty of Malaysia, Vietnam, and Singapore. Travel has served as a way to follow an expanding horizon. With the broadening of horizons, there also came a deepening of understanding, appreciation, and profound thanksgiving for God's beautiful creation.

Food and Drink

No doubt about it, Jim loved to eat. A Southerner, he believed with all of his heart that pork barbeque was the greatest gift of God to humankind, followed closely by a good marbled steak. Jim loved oilcloth–covered tables in small-town joints as much as the finest uptown restaurants. He believed that no day should be wasted without the enjoyment of food.

Even after his first heart attack, when Jim learned to eat right, he still allowed himself a little bending room and an occasional cholesterol binge. He believed that contentment contributed to good health. Though willing to give up cigarettes completely and without fail, his favorite foods—in proper proportions—remained on Jim's menu.

Though a Baptist to the end of his days, Jim followed the example of Jesus and on occasion enjoyed good wine, and a nip of Black Label Jack Daniels put a smile on Jim's Tennessee face. He never gave up his SAE heritage and loved a good party!

Architectural Beauty

Perhaps in his next life, Jim will be a structural or landscape architect. When Jim needed to feed his soul, he would mow his lawn, prune roses, or tend his garden. He loved a well-designed yard, a preserved and ancient tree, a moss-covered brick sidewalk, and a freshly painted fence. Life was in order when Jim's yard was in order.

Jim also appreciated a well-designed house. Shortly before his death, Jim and Carolyn designed a house on Seabrook Island that captured their artistic taste and Southern heritage. It is a creation of craft and beauty. Jim died after living in this house for only a few weeks, but his spirit remains there and can be seen in the stately columns, the perfect symmetry, and the broad porches that surround the house, offering friendship and hospitality to all who sit in its shade. Jim loved architectural beauty and a life that exhibited artistic graciousness.

The life of Jim McAfee cannot be captured by the limited words of this chapter but only suggested by the few broad themes presented here. His life-dream was multi-faceted, and it can best be seen by the convergence and balance of his vocation, his core beliefs, his relationships, and his avocational pursuits.

Far better than most, Jim understood his life-dream, achieved his goals, and lived an authentic and productive life. Unlike most, however, Jim and Carolyn McAfee shared with others in a rare and extravagant way. In the words of Dr. Kirby Godsey, "The McAfees are the most generous people I know. They had the gift of giving. They had the capacity to see beyond themselves and to engage in true stewardship." This was the McAfee gift. This is their legacy.

Notes

Chapter 1

[1] Maria T. Daviess, *History of Mercer and Boyle Counties*, vol. 1 (Harrodsburg KY: Harrodsburg Herald, 1924; reprinted 1962).

[2] Jenny Tenlen, "The McAfees: Kentucky Pioneers," 1 January 2011, http://jtenlen.drizzlehosting.com/Register/RR_TOC.HTML (accessed 23 October 2010); Robert Morgan, *Boone: A Biography* (Chapel Hill NC: Algonquin Books, Reprinted 2008); "The History of the McAfee-Waddell-Allen Families," unpublished manuscript in possession of J. Thomas McAfee, III.

[3] William Cleveland McAfee, born 9 October 1884 and died 28 April 1955. Hattie May Price McAfee, born February 11, 1883 and died January 19, 1956.

[4] No McAfee families are listed in federal censuses as living in Dyer County, Tennessee, prior to 1910.

[5] Dyer County, Tennessee, Census Report, 1930.

[6] J. Thomas McAfee, III, interview by author, August 4, 2010.

[7] Ibid.

[8] Ibid.

[9] Ibid.

[10] Ibid.

[11] Ibid.

[12] Civil War military records for Joseph Hilliard, files.usgwarchives.net/al/madison/military/civilwar/other/somecivi502gmt.txt.

[13] C. D. Hilliard, interview by author, January 5, 2011.

[14] Carolyn Townsend McAfee, interview by author, July 13, 2010.

Chapter 2

[1] J. Thomas McAfee, III, interview by author, 4 August 2010.

[2] Matthew 5:8.

[3] J. Thomas McAfee, III, interview by author, August 4, 2010.

---

[4] Carolyn Townsend McAfee and Diane Hill, interview by author, January 23-24, 2010.

Chapter 3

[1] Jackson, Tennessee, had a population of approximately 25,000 people in 1945.

[2] J. Thomas McAfee, III, interview by author, August 4, 2010.

[3] Matt Tomlin, interview by author, December 14, 2010.

[4] J. Thomas McAfee, III, interview by author, August 4, 2010; Carolyn Townsend McAfee, interview by author, July 13, 2010.

[5] Diane Harding Hill, interview by author, January 23, 2010.

[6] Carolyn Townsend McAfee, interview by author, July 13, 2010.

[7] J. Thomas McAfee, III, interview by author, August 4, 2010.

[8] Carolyn Townsend McAfee, interview by author, July 13, 2010.

[9] J. Thomas McAfee, III, interview by author, July 13, 2010; Hyran Barefoot, interview by author, 28 October 2010; Kirby Godsey, interview by author, July 14, 2010.

[10] J. Thomas McAfee, III, interview by author, July 13, 2010.

[11] Kirby Godsey, interview by author, July 14, 2010.

[12] J. Thomas McAfee, III, interview by author, August 4, 2010; Hyran Barefoot, interview by author, October 28, 2010.

[13] J. Thomas McAfee, III, interview by author, August 4, 2010.

[14] Hampton Williams, interview by author, June 5, 2011.

[15] Ibid.; J. Thomas McAfee, III, interview by author, August 4, 2010; Hyran Barefoot, interview by author, October 28, 2011; Carolyn Townsend McAfee, July 13, 2010.

Chapter 4

[1] US Census of Population, 1950, vol. II, "Characteristics of the Population," Part 42, Tennessee, Chapter B, 32. US Government Printing Office, Washington DC, 1952.

[2] Hampton Williams, interview by author, June 5, 2010.

[3] Bob Haynie, interview by author, June 8, 2011; Matt Tomlin, interview by author, 14 December, 2010.

[4] Matt Tomlin, interview by author, December 14, 2010.

[5] Ibid.

[6] Bob Haynie, interview by author, June 8, 2011.

[7] Ibid.
[8] Ibid.
[9] Matt Tomlin, interview by author, December 14, 2010.
[10] J. Thomas McAfee, III, interview by author, August 4, 2010.
[11] Matt Tomlin, interview by author, December 14, 2010; Hampton Williams, interview by author, June 5, 2011; Bob Haynie, interview by author, June 14, 2011.
[12] Matt Tomlin, interview by author, December 14, 2010.
[13] Ibid.; Hampton Williams, interview by author, June 5, 2011; Bob Haynie, interview by author, June 8, 2011.
[14] J. Thomas McAfee, III, interview by author, August 4, 2010.

Chapter 5

[1] David Reynolds, *America, Empire of Liberty* (New York: Basic Books, 2009) 339, 368.
[2] J. Thomas McAfee, III, interview by author, August 4, 2010; Carolyn Townsend McAfee, interview by author, July 13, 2010.
[3] Nick Ravo, "John Tigrett, 85, Entrepreneur and Inventor in Tennessee," http://www.nytimes.com/1999/05/27/business/john-tigrett-85-entrepreneur-and-inventor-in-tennessee.html (accessed 6/3/2104).
[4] Ibid.
[5] J. Thomas McAfee, III, interview by author, August 4, 2010; Carolyn Townsend McAfee, interview by author, July 13, 2010; Nick Ravo, "John Tigrett, 85, Entrepreneur and Inventor in Tennessee."
[6] Nathan Pillow, interview by author, October 28, 2010.
[7] J. Thomas McAfee, III, interview by author, August 4, 2010; Nathan Pillow, interview by author, October 28, 2010.
[8] Carolyn Townsend McAfee, interview by author, July 13, 2010.
[9] Hyran Barefoot, interview by author, October 28, 2010; Hyran Barefoot, "Famous Last Words," *The Unionite,* http://www.uu.edu?Unionite/SUMMER96/famous.htm (accessed October 27, 2010).
[10] Nathan Pillow, interview by author, October 28, 2010.
[11] Ibid.
[12] J. Thomas McAfee, III, interview by author, August 4, 2010.
[13] Nathan Pillow, interview by author, October 28, 2010.
[14] Matt Tomlin, interview by author, December 14, 2010.

Chapter 6

[1] The primary source of information in this chapter is from interviews by the author with Carolyn Townsend McAfee, July19 and 28, 2010.

[2] Carolyn Townsend McAfee, interview by author, July 28, 2011.

[1] Bob Jeffries, interview by author, July 18, 2011.

[2] Ibid.

[3] Calvin Harrell, email communication, April 14, 2009.

[4] Ibid.

[5] Carolyn Townsend McAfee, interview by author, 28 July 2011.

[6] Ibid.

[7] Ibid.

[8] Ibid.

Chapter 7

[1] Robbie Prince Andrews, interview with author, February 13, 2012.

[2] Harold and Jeanette Haney, interview with author, February 8, 2012.

[3] Jack R. Anderson, interview with author, July 1, 2012.

[4] George Shaunnessey, interview with author, June 20, 2012.

[5] J. Thomas McAfee, III. and Carolyn Townsend McAfee, interview by author, March 7, 2012.

Chapter 8

[1] Jim Buncher, interview by author, July 15, 2011.

[2] Ibid.

[3] Ibid.

[4] Carolyn Townsend McAfee, interview with author, March 7, 2012.

[5] J. Thomas McAfee, III, interview with author, March 7, 2012.

[6] Carolyn Townsend McAfee, interview with author, July 10, 2012.

Chapter 9

[1] "William Arthur Fickling, Sr., Made Macon, Georgia, the Cherry Tree Capital," *Los Angeles Times,* November 7, 1990.

[2] William A. Fickling, Jr., interview by author, 12 March 2012; "Miss America", http://www.missamerica.org/our-miss-americas/1950/1953.aspx. June 11, 2012.

---

[3] J. Thomas McAfee, III, interview by author, March 7, 2012.

[4] William A. Fickling, Jr., interview by author, March 12, 2012.

[5] J. Thomas McAfee, III, interview by author, March 7, 2012.

[6] Carolyn Townsend McAfee, interview by author, March 7, 2012.

[7] George Shaunnessy, interview by author, June 20, 2012.

[8] Ronald W. Manderschied and Marilyn J. Henderson, eds., *Mental Health, United States, 1998* (Rockville MA: United States Department of Health and Human Services, 1998) 143–45.

[9] Kay W. Slayden, interview by author, July 23, 2012.

[10] He was listed at number 245.

[11] "Forbes 400 List of Wealthiest Americans," http://www.apnew-archive.com/1987/Forbes-400 (accessed June 1, 2014).

[12] Kirby Godsey, interview by author, July 14, 2010.

[13] Isaac Watts, "O God, Our Help in Ages Past," *Celebrating Grace* (Macon GA: Celebrating Grace, Inc., 2010) 566.

[14] William A. Fickling, Jr., interview by author, March 12, 2012.

[15] Carolyn Townsend McAfee and J. Thomas McAfee, III, interview by author, March 7, 2012.

[16] Ibid.

[17] Hyran Barefoot, interview by author, October 28, 2010.

[18] George Shaunnessy, interview by author, June 20, 2012.

[19] Carolyn Townsend McAfee, interview by author, October 18, 2011.

[20] Carolyn Townsend McAfee, interview by author, October 18, 2011 and 14 March 2012.

[21] J. Thomas McAfee, III, interview by author, March 14 and 26, 2012.

[22] Carolyn Townsend McAfee, interview by author, March 14 and 26, 2012.

[23] J. Thomas McAfee, III. and Julie Crangle McAfee, interview by author, March 12, 2012.

[24] J. Thomas McAfee, III, interview by author, March 12 and 26, 2012.

[25] Thomas B. Walters, *Charles T. Studd: Cricketer and Missionary* (London: Epworth Press, 1930).

[26] Carolyn Townsend McAfee and J. Thomas McAfee, III, interview by author, March 14 and 26, 2012.

[27] Ibid.

[28] Ibid.

Chapter 10

[1] J. Thomas McAfee, III, interview by author, March 14 and 26, 2012.
[2] Kay Slayden, interview by author, July 23, 2012.
[3] George Shaunnessey, interview by author, June 20, 2012; J. Thomas McAfee, III, interview by author, March 14, 2012.
[4] J. Thomas McAfee, III, interview by author, March 14 and 26, 2012.
[5] George Shaunnessey, interview by author, June 20, 2012.
[6] J. Thomas McAfee, III, interview by author, August 24, 2012.
[7] Hyran Barefoot, interview by author, October 28, 2010.
[8] J. Thomas McAfee, III, interview by author, August 24, 2012.
[9] Carolyn Townsend McAfee, interview by author, April 12, 2012.
[10] J. Thomas McAfee, III, interview by author, August 24, 2012.
[11] Ibid.
[12] J. Thomas McAfee, III, interview by author, April 19, 2012.
[13] Ibid.
[14] Julie Crangle McAfee, interview by author, April 19, 2012.
[15] J. Thomas McAfee, III. and Julie Crangle McAfee, interview by author, April 9, 2012.
[16] Julie Crangle McAfee, interview by author, April 23, 2012.

Chapter 11

[1] Robert Miller, interview by author, May 22, 2012.
[2] Kay W. Slayden, interview by author, July 23, 2011.
[3] Ibid.
[4] Kirby Godsey, interview by author, July 14, 2010.
[5] James G. Shoopman, ed., *The Fundamentalist Takeover in the Southern Baptist Convention,* 3rd ed., http://www.sbctakeover.com/chapter21.htm (accessed 2 October 2010).
[6] John Pierce, interview by author, July 25, 2012.
[7] J. Thomas McAfee, III. and Carolyn Townsend McAfee, interview by author, April 12, 2012.
[8] Kirby Godsey, interview by author, July 14, 2010.
[9] Alan Culpepper, interview by author, September 11, 2012.
[10] Ibid.
[11] Ibid.
[12] Emily Myers, *Mercer Theology Update* 10, 3 (Fall 2004): 1.

[13] Robert Penn Warren, "Reading Late at Night, Thermometer Falling," in *New and Selected Poems: 1923–1985* (Franklin Center PA: Franklin Library, 1985) 200–05.

[14] Hyran Barefoot, interview by author, October 28, 2010.

[15] Thornton Wilder, *Our Town: A Play In Three Acts* (New York: Harper Collins, 1938, 2003) 87–88.

Chapter 12

[1] Alan Culpepper, interview by author, 11 September 2012; Kirby Godsey, interview by author, July 14, 2010.

[2] J. Thomas McAfee, III. and Carolyn Townsend McAfee, interview by author, March 26 and April 12, 2012.

[3] Ibid.

[4] Kirby Godsey, Eulogy for James T. McAfee, Jr., quoted in *Mercer Theology Update*, published by the McAfee School of Theology, Mercer University (November 2004).

[5] Psalm 121.

[6] William Penn, quoted in George Anderson, ed., *The Oxford Book of Prayer* (Oxford: University Press, 1985) 63.

Chapter 13

[1] Tom McAfee, interview by author, March 5, 2014.

[2] Carolyn McAfee, interview by author, March 17, 2014.

[3] Tom and Carolyn McAfee, interview by author, March 17, 2014.

[4] Tom McAfee. Personal files.

Chapter 14

[1] Daniel J. Levinson, et al., *The Seasons of a Man's Life* (New York: Alfred A. Knopf, Inc., 1978), pp. 91-97.

[2] Marcus Buckingham and Donald O. Clifton, *Now, Discover Your Strengths* (New York: The Free Press, 2001).

[3] Ibid., 32.

[4] Mark: 12:28-31.

[5] Steve Saint, *End of the Spear* (Carol Stream, IL: Tyndale House, 2005).

[6] George Shaunnessey, interview by author, June 20, 2012.

---

[7] William A. Fickling, Jr., interview by author, March 12, 2012.
[8] Matt Tomlin, December 14, 2010.
[9] Kirby Godsey, interview by author, July 14, 2010.
[10] Tom McAfee, interview by author, April 23, 2012.
[11] Julie McAfee, interview by author, April 23, 2012.
[12] Nathan Pillow, interview by author, October 28, 2010.
[13] Bob Jeffries, interview by author, July 18, 2011.
[14] Calvin Harrell, letter to Carolyn McAfee, April 14, 2009.

Index